SERVICE IN A TIME OF SUSPICION

SERVICE IN A TIME OF SUSPICION

Experiences of Muslims Serving

in the U.S. Military Post-9/11

MICHELLE SANDHOFF

University of Iowa Press, Iowa City

University of Iowa Press, Iowa City 52242

Copyright © 2017 by the University of Iowa Press

www.uipress.uiowa.edu

Printed in the United States of America

Design by Ashley Muehlbauer

The University of Iowa Press is a member of Green Press Initiative and is committed to preserving natural resources.

Printed on acid-free paper

ISBN: 978-1-60938-535-4 (pbk)

ISBN: 978-1-60938-536-1 (ebk)

Library of Congress Cataloging-in-Publication Data is on file at the Library of Congress.

To all who serve with the recognition
that service comes in many forms

CONTENTS

ACKNOWLEDGMENTS

The final form of this project represents not just the labor of many years, but also the contributions and support of an entire community. I extend my heartfelt thanks to everyone who helped make this project a reality.

I would like to start by thanking the editors and reviewers who saw potential in this project and provided me with feedback to improve it. In particular, thanks to Kim Hansen who has provided guidance, advice, and a willing ear from the very beginning of this project.

My thanks are also due to my doctoral dissertation advisor, David R. Segal, whose support, not just through the process of writing the dissertation which led to this book, but throughout my years as a graduate student, has been invaluable. Thank you for your mentorship and your encouragement.

I would also like to thank the other members of my dissertation committee: Meyer Kestnbaum, Meredith Kleykamp, Kris Marsh, and Michael Paolisso, who provided their insight and guidance throughout this project. The final product would not be what it is without your thoughtful input. I would particularly like to thank Meredith Kleykamp, who was always willing to help me sort out my thoughts when I got lost in the frustration of collecting data or tangled in an analysis.

I owe Mady Wechsler Segal more than I can express here. You have taught me much of what I know about diversity in the military, and without your guidance I would not be the scholar, or the person, I am today.

A big thank-you to my colleagues for sharing the ups and downs of this journey with me. In particular, Karin DeAngelis, Michelle Smirnova, and Kim Hansen, your support and company throughout this process have been invaluable. I can honestly say this project would not have come to fruition without you. I look forward to many years of continued friendship and collaboration with you.

Armaghan Naik, thank you for the hours you spent helping me brainstorm and work through how to organize and conceptualize this project. To Katie Mapes, who was always willing to lend an ear to listen to both elation and frustration during the course of this project, thank you for your support.

To everyone who helped me find participants, especially Farah Mahesri, know that quite literally this project is a result of your generosity and assistance.

I would also like to thank the University of Iowa Press for encouraging me to transform my doctoral dissertation into this book. In particular I would like to thank my editors, Elisabeth Chretien and Catherine Cocks, the anonymous reviewers who provided valuable feedback, and my copyeditor Paul Mendelson.

Finally, to the service members who participated in this project—I am honored that you chose to share your stories with me and hope that the following pages do justice to your experiences. Thank you for your generosity in taking time out of your busy lives to share your stories with me.

INTRODUCTION

On September 11, 2001, four passenger jets were hijacked and flown into the World Trade Center and the Pentagon (and the fourth intended for another target in Washington, DC) in a coordinated terrorist attack that killed almost 3,000 people. It was an unprecedented act of terror on American soil, and defined the new century as the United States struggled to find a balance between national security and civil rights while engaged in what became long-lasting, unconventional wars in Afghanistan and Iraq. The events of 9/11 and the subsequent "War on Terror" reinvigorated long-standing stereotypes in the United States that portrayed Muslims as fundamentally different from other Americans. Within this context, thousands of Muslims chose to serve in the U.S. armed forces. In this book I consider the experiences of some of these Muslim service members.

I began my first year of college about a week after the 9/11 attacks, and this historical moment has shaped many of my experiences both educational and personal; perhaps it is this context that sparked my interest in studying the military and war. I came of age in a time period that straddled two different eras, marked both by the new millennium and by the dramatic changes 9/11 wrought on U.S. society. As a white woman, the post-9/11 environment had few direct effects on me other than having to take my shoes off at the airport; however, I was fortunate enough to grow up with a diverse set of friends who were willing to share their experiences and observations with me. Through them, I was able to hear about and see how the divisions sparked by 9/11 shaped the experiences of people who did not look like me.

All of this background came together in one of those lightbulb-over-head moments as I was struggling to figure out what I wanted to commit several years to studying to complete my doctoral degree in military sociology at the University of Maryland. When I began this project in 2009, I was shocked to find so little material out there about the experiences of Muslims in the U.S. military, and I set out to start collecting and sharing these stories. There is still far too little data and far too many assumptions about this population, and it is my hope that the stories I will share in the following pages will help ignite an interest in getting beyond stereotypes to hear what these service members and veterans have to say.

BEING MUSLIM IN THE UNITED STATES AFTER 9/11

After 9/11, being Muslim American became complicated. The FBI documented a dramatic increase in hate crimes targeting Muslims following 9/11. Anti-Islamic hate crimes remain about three times as frequent as they were prior to 9/11.[1] In public policy, Muslims became a population of interest. No-fly lists and watch lists filled up with Muslim names. In 2012 the Associated Press won a Pulitzer Prize for a series of investigative reports documenting the systematic monitoring of mosques, Muslim businesses, and student groups by the New York Police Department (NYPD).[2]

Being Muslim became a source of suspicion. A geographically, racially, and culturally diverse population came to be primarily identifiable by a shared label: Muslim. And that label came with sometimes serious consequences. Several scholars have explored the experiences of Muslims living in the United States in a post-9/11 world. The sociologist Lori Peek interviewed Muslim college and university students living in New York City following 9/11; respondents reported negative responses ranging "from stares and 'nasty looks' to verbal harassment and even physical assault."[3] Her respondents felt like they were suddenly treated as outsiders and were regarded with suspicion and fear. One respondent recalled, "Before this [9/11] happened, I felt like this is my country. I belong here. Now going outside, I feel like, I'm sorry, I shouldn't be here. It's a problem I'm here. I really feel like I should go somewhere else."[4]

The post-9/11 world is a complicated space for American Muslims. Following the attacks, a narrative arose that "othered" Muslims, treating them as different from, and more dangerous than, other Americans. Following 9/11, the idea that being a "good" Muslim and a "good" American are impossible at the same time became very common. From the variously expressed sentiment that Muslims "go back home," to formal congressional hearings on the radicalization of Muslim Americans, to references to the "clash of civilizations" theory,[5] the idea that it is impossible to be both American and Muslim is pervasive. Slecuk Sirin and Michelle Fine argue:

> Unfortunately, oblivious to the distinctions and variations within the Muslim community and with no attention to language, the media produce, legitimate, and circulate stereotypes like this one about Muslim Americans as binaries. We could easily dismiss these statements as extreme ideas put forward by a minority, but unfortunately these views are common on TV and talk radio and in print.[6]

The reality, of course, is more complex, and many Muslims in the United States see American and Muslim as compatible identities. However, even in these cases, the expectations from others that they must choose or prioritize one identity over the other may shape their experience.

THE MILITARY CONTEXT

Within the post-9/11 context, thousands of Muslims joined the U.S. military. The U.S. military has a long and complicated history with questions of who is and is not an "American." This relationship has two components. One of the connections between the military and citizenship is that military service, especially during times of war, can lead to increased citizenship rights. That is, when members of a disadvantaged group serve in the military, they may be able to use this service to claim fuller citizenship rights. Another connection between the military and citizenship is that the right to serve in the military is itself an indicator of citizenship. For example, the political scientist Ronald Krebs notes, "Participation in the armed forces has, at least in the nation-state system, been depicted as a sign of one's full membership in the political community as well as evidence of one's worthiness for membership."[7] Being allowed to serve indicates you are seen as belonging to the nation, while serving can prove your worthiness to belong. The role of military service as an indicator of inclusion can be seen in the reluctance to include marginalized minority groups in the military. Historically, the exclusion of marginalized groups from military service has been connected to a reluctance to recognize them as full citizens; in the United States, military service has been contested for African Americans, Native Americans, women, and LGBT (lesbian, gay, bisexual, and transgender) individuals, among others.[8] Being included in the military is a powerful indicator that you are seen as a member of the nation and you have the right (and duty) to defend it.

Military service has also been used to make citizenship claims. Military service, and the risks it entails, is often seen as a way to prove loyalty and worthiness for full citizenship. In 1862 the U.S. Congress first passed legislation granting expedited naturalization for immigrants who served in the U.S. military. Despite this, after World War I, Asian veterans were often denied citizenship because of their race.[9] However, military service ultimately won out, and the passage of the Nye-Lea Act in 1935 allowed Asian veterans to naturalize almost twenty years before other Asian immigrants were able to become U.S. citizens.[10]

During the internment of Japanese in America during World War II, military service was also a contested topic. At first Japanese Americans were explicitly excluded from military conscription: Nisei—second-generation Japanese Americans—were classified as "aliens ineligible for military service." In 1943, however, a special combat unit composed exclusively of Japanese Americans was formed, in part as a way for Japanese Americans to demonstrate their loyalty.[11] The exemplary record of the 442nd Regimental Combat Team and their recognition in American popular culture helped facilitate the integration of Japanese Americans into the American mainstream.[12]

During the 2016 presidential race similar themes were raised. Khizr Khan, a lawyer from Maryland whose son, Humayun Khan, was a U.S. Army captain killed in Iraq, gave a speech at the Democratic National Convention with some familiar themes. Khan described his family as "patriotic American Muslims with undivided loyalty to our country," implicitly responding to the stereotypes that pose Muslim and American as incompatible identities. He connected the idea of sacrifice through military service to ideas of citizenship and belonging: "Have you ever been to Arlington Cemetery? Go look at the graves of brave patriots who died defending the United States of America."[13] Ghazala Khan, the mother of Humayun, continued the themes of sacrifice in an op-ed she wrote for the *Washington Post*: "It has been 12 years, but you know hearts of pain can never heal as long as we live. Just talking about it is hard for me all the time. Every day, whenever I pray, I have to pray for him, and I cry. The place that emptied will always be empty."[14] Presidential candidate Donald Trump responded with what the *New York Times* characterized as a "rough and ethnically charged dismissal" and "religious stereotypes."[15]

THIS PROJECT

The military is a prominent social institution in America.[16] At the same time, much of the American media frames Muslims as fundamentally un-American. I wanted to know what the experience was like for Muslim service members who inhabited the space between these ideas.

The military is a compelling space to examine the experiences of Muslim Americans because of its history with diversity. The military has in some ways mitigated the negative effects of discrimination in the civilian world through policies and regulations designed to emphasize equality of opportunity. For example, racial integration is often hailed as an area where the military has excelled at promoting diversity. At the same time, the military is also a social institution that has not just accepted, but has for many years enshrined in policy, stereotypes about women and the LGBT community that led to exclusion and even violence within the ranks. Add to all this the current conflicts with U.S. troops serving in predominantly Muslim countries against an enemy often characterized as "Islamic."

This mixed history and context left me with an interesting puzzle. In the case of Muslim Americans serving in the post-9/11 world, would the military provide a protective environment or a problematic one? Would I find a repeat of the stereotypes and negative ideas so common in civilian society, or would I find Muslim service members who were fully included? In this book I will show that, at least among the people who spoke with me, there was some of both. Differences in unit-level leadership and conditions created varied experiences. For some people, the military provided a stable job with opportunity for advancement. For those who had negative encounters with colleagues, there was a clear process to address these issues. However, some people shared experiences where weak leadership fostered climates of distrust and suspicion. In these units they felt singled out, excluded, and degraded. In total, ten of the people who spoke with me had generally positive experiences in the military, three had generally negative experiences in the military, and two had a mix of positive and negative experiences.

A few factors structured whether someone had positive or negative experiences. An important element in the stories that people shared with me was the structure of the military, particularly the enforcement of equal opportunity policies and the existence of offices and advisors to help them address any problems that arose. Another factor was the practical relevance of diversity in the field. All of the people who spoke with me who served on the ground in Iraq or Afghanistan found their identity and background to be a valuable resource. This everyday proof (to themselves, their colleagues, and their commanders) of the value of diversity tended to shape positive experiences. Another factor was leadership, a specific part of the military structure. Good leadership appears in many of the stories of the people who had positive experiences. They felt they were supported and appreciated and the units they served in were cohesive and unified. But leadership also appears at the heart of most of the negative experiences that people had. In these cases, leaders who were suspicious of Muslims or critical of diversity more broadly failed to create cohesive units, and within these settings, the people who spoke with me did not thrive. Two other factors came up among those respondents who had negative experiences: one was the exclusion of any discussion of Islam from advanced language training, and the other was the endangerment of family due to service in a war zone.

COLLECTING STORIES

The interviews for this book were conducted with Muslim service members and veterans who have served in the U.S. military since 9/11. I conducted interviews from June 2010 through December 2011. In total, fifteen people agreed to share their stories with me. These respondents came from a variety of backgrounds and have served throughout the U.S. military. I found people willing to talk with me via personal contacts, flyers, electronic discussion lists, and word of mouth.

In collecting these stories, I was looking for people who self-identify as Muslim and have served for a period of time in the U.S. armed forces since September 2001. I did not limit the sample by service branch, and I accepted respondents who served in the National Guard and the reserves. I spoke with both veterans and current service members.

The label *Muslim* encompasses a very diverse population. Muslims in the United States come from a variety of racial and ethnic backgrounds, are of various socioeconomic classes, and have diverse personal and family backgrounds and characteristics. While it is not useful to speak of one homogenous "Muslim perspective," I was interested in common challenges associated with this shared identity. I therefore focus on self-identification as "Muslim." It is important to distinguish identifying as Muslim from practicing Islam. The people who spoke with me included individuals who identified as Muslim due to religious practice, family history, and conversion. In terms of religiosity, my sample covered the spectrum from atheistic to pious. I did not ask respondents about their denominational affiliation (e.g., Sunni, Shia) because this is not relevant to my research questions. I spoke with both individuals who were born into Muslim families and those who converted to Islam. The inclusion of converts gives a fairer picture of the U.S. Muslim population. According to the Pew Research Center's 2011 report,[17] the American Muslim community is comprised of 20 percent converts. Interestingly, for three of the converts I spoke with (Daniel, Omar, and Rahma), Islam was something they began to explore in response to specific experiences in the military.

When I asked respondents about their religious practice they tended to categorize themselves based on practices such as praying, fasting, and dietary restrictions. For example, Kareem (chapter 3) reported:

> I wasn't a very good Muslim on active duty. I didn't pray five times a day. That's really the only thing that I didn't really observe. I didn't really drink [alcohol], I didn't eat pork, I fasted Ramadan.[18]

In chapter 2 I will discuss the ritual practices of prayer and fasting within the military context.

THE STORYTELLERS

The Muslim service members and veterans who spoke with me were a diverse group both in terms of demographic characteristics and military background. They were predominantly male (13). Ethnically, most identified as South Asian (8), though I also spoke with white (3), Arab (2), and multiracial (2) respondents. I did not find any differences in experiences associated with ethnicity. This could be because after 9/11 religious identity came to outweigh ethnic identity. It could also be due to the way this diverse group may be seen by others as ethnically homogenous. Although they come from various ethnic and national backgrounds, several noted the ways in which people made incorrect assumptions about their ancestry or thought that categories such as Arab and South Asian were interchangeable. It could also be the case that with a larger sample, more differences would arise. Most of the people who spoke with me either immigrated to the United States or were the children of immigrants.

The individuals who spoke with me had varied military experiences. Most were no longer serving in the military when we spoke. I talked to people from every service branch except the Coast Guard. The branches with the largest number of respondents were the Navy (5) and Air Force (5), followed by the Army (4) and only one person who served in the Marine Corps. The people who spoke with me were at different points in their careers when they left the military (or at the time of interview). Most had served fewer than 20 years; however, 4 had served 20 years or more. Among those who had left the military, the shortest career was 4 years, the longest 24 years. The average length of service for those who had left the military was 10.7 years. Most of the people I spoke with were enlisted men or women (9) as opposed to officers. Five had deployed to Iraq or Afghanistan, and 3 were in combat positions.

LIMITATIONS

This book offers a glimpse into the world of Muslim service members, but it is not an exhaustive study. The stories of the fifteen people I share here weave together a set of themes that I will highlight in the coming chapters, but do not represent the entirety of the experience of being Muslim in the military. In other words, as a qualitative study with exploratory goals, the data presented here are not generalizable and should not be taken as representative of the experiences of all Muslim service members.

There are also two important populations that are missing from this study: black Muslims and Muslims "passing" as non-Muslim. Although African Americans are estimated to comprise almost half of all Muslims in the military,[19] there is no one in this study who identifies as exclusively black. I did not intentionally exclude this population. That this group either did not hear about this study or chose not to participate is an interesting topic worthy of future investigation. This absence makes it impossible to determine whether or not being labeled or identified as Muslim transcends race. Another population that is missing from my sample are those who "pass" as non-Muslim. It is clear that this population does exist; however, they are unlikely to participate in a study such as this because participating carries the risk of "outing" themselves. The people whose stories I relate here are all known to be Muslim by their colleagues.

CONFIDENTIALITY

All names used for respondents are pseudonyms. Pseudonyms were selected with the goal of being distinct and easy to remember for the reader, and moreover, they have no relation to the name or ethnicity of the respondent.

Given the small number of Muslims in the U.S. military, relatively minor details could be used to identify these individuals. I have therefore masked certain details, including any indication of the military branch the person served in. Aggregated totals can be found in this introduction, but all identifiers of service branch in the stories themselves have been replaced with generics (such as "military"). In order to maintain the flow of the narratives, in most cases I have not marked where I have made such changes.

I have also obscured the origins of my respondents by aggregating specific ancestries into the pan-ethnic terms of *South Asian* and *Arab* unless there is a need to indicate a specific country or language. When I use these terms, they are accurate reflections of the individual's background, but are intentionally imprecise. As with military branch, I have replaced specific references in the narratives with a generic term.

ORGANIZATION OF THIS BOOK

I have organized this book around the stories of fifteen people. I present the experiences of each person using his or her own words. Although fifteen individuals are represented here, I tell sixteen stories, because I have divided the experiences of one respondent into two sections for confidentiality reasons. I have grouped these individual stories in a way designed to draw out common themes and to allow comparisons across cases.

I begin, in chapter 1, with an examination of Muslims in the United States. This chapter begins with a brief overview of the history of Muslims in the United States. I then consider the historical and contemporary ways in which Muslims have been and are treated as outsiders in the West. I look in particular at the rise of Islamophobia following 9/11 and throughout the contemporary period.

In chapter 2, I explore diversity in the military. I briefly discuss the history of the integration of African Americans, women, and LGBT individuals into the U.S. military. I then consider some of the characteristics of the military that shape diversity and integration; the case study of Japanese American service members during World War II is considered. In this chapter, I also provide an overview of what is known about Muslims in the military. Finally, I make a case for the importance of diversity to the military.

In chapter 3, I use four very different stories to introduce the reader to the range of experiences of Muslims in the military. I begin by sharing Mahmood's story since his experiences were quite similar to those of many of the other people who spoke with me, and this serves as a useful starting point. Next, Sadia relates her story, which is filled with suspicion and a formal investigation. I return to the positive with Kareem, who began serving before 9/11 and sees a culture shift in the military around diversity issues. I conclude this chapter with a look at Farid, who shared with me the most tragic experience I heard during this project.

I consider the central role of leadership in shaping the experiences of service members in chapter 4. As with chapter 3, I alternate between positive and negative experiences to give the reader a sense of the range of experiences. I present the stories of two individuals, Tarek and Najib, where strong leadership created positive environments. I also present the stories of Zafir and Basim, who had negative experiences related to weak or problematic leadership.

In chapter 5, I explore the role of diversity in military education and experience. I begin with the stories of Omar and Daniel, two respondents who do not know each other, but who had very similar experiences while in the military that taken together suggest a pattern of problems in language training. I then share the stories of Pervez and Jamal, two respondents who used their identities and backgrounds to help achieve the mission on the ground in Afghanistan.

In chapter 6, I consider some of the ways in which the people I spoke with explored their identities as Muslim American service members. I introduce Yusuf, who has used his religious faith to make sense of his combat experiences; Rahma, who sees herself as a bridge builder; and Hakim, who is outspoken and more than willing to stand up for his rights and the rights of other Muslims in the U.S. military.

In chapter 7, I consider the themes that emerged in the preceding chapters and ask what we can learn from the experiences of Muslim Americans in the military.

EDITING AND TERMINOLOGY

I have done minor cosmetic editing to some of the narratives to enhance readability. If substantial text was removed I indicate this with [. . .]. Ellipses without brackets indicate that the text is intact, but signal a noticeable pause and often a switch of topic.

When using non-English terms, I use the transliteration that I expect will be the most familiar to the readers. For example, I use the spelling Osama bin

Laden although Usama is a more accurate transliteration. I use both the spellings Qur'an and Koran in reference to the Islamic sacred text. I use the spelling Koran when I am quoting a source that uses this spelling. I also use this spelling to signal that a respondent has intentionally mispronounced the word to convey ignorance or maliciousness.

ONE

BEING MUSLIM IN
THE UNITED STATES

Fear and even hatred of Islam and Muslims is not a new phenomenon caused by 9/11, but rather the reinvigoration of prejudices and fears that likely traveled to American shores with the first European colonizers. The historian Denise Spellberg observed that "it is notable how much the anti-Islamic invective inflamed by 9/11 resembles the denigration of Islam in America as far back as the seventeenth century."[1] Other scholars trace the roots of contemporary fears about Islam even further, arguing that today's stereotypes can be traced to the Middle Ages. Since its beginning in the seventh century AD, Islam was perceived as a threat to predominantly Christian Europe. Islam was seen as a false religion, and the military might of the Islamic Empire posed a very real threat to Europe. From their earliest encounters with each other, the West viewed Islam as an existential threat. Centuries of warfare honed these negative narratives and embedded them deep within Western thought.[2] The historian Norman Daniel explored the development of Christian European approaches to Islam in the thirteenth and fourteenth centuries, arguing that contemporary approaches to Islam are heirs to this legacy: "the style of the day changes, but the themes are perennial."[3] The communications scholar Karim H. Karim argues that negative stereotypes about Muslims can be seen in the works of Beethoven, Dante, Mozart, Shakespeare, and Voltaire and that as these artists' classics are revisited in each generation, they "[sustain] a world view in which 'Mohammadens' are essentially gripped by violence, lust, greed, and barbarism."[4]

During the Protestant Reformation of the sixteenth century, Islam was commonly associated with the Antichrist. Martin Luther and John Calvin both argued that the Antichrist was a dual enemy composed of Catholicism and Islam. Catholics also held Islam in contempt, often negatively comparing Protestantism to Islam.[5] This fear of Islam largely stemmed from concern over the military might of the Ottoman Empire, which conquered southeastern Europe and even besieged Vienna.

During the founding of the United States, Islam was used as a hypothetical test case for religious freedom precisely because it was viewed so negatively. Muslims, along with Catholics and Jews, were considered outsiders by the Protestant founders of the United States. At the time the Constitution was written, it was common for state officials to be required to undergo a "religious test," which was designed to exclude all but Protestants from holding public office. In debating whether such a test should be included in the Constitution (it was not), the founders referred frequently to the hypothetical example of Muslims, who were seen by many at the time as the epitome of theological and political corruption.[6]

Although the Founding Fathers debated the role of Muslims as a hypothetical exercise, the first Muslims had already arrived in America. Among the slaves brought to the American Colonies and then the United States in the eighteenth century, as many as 10 percent were Muslim,[7] and Muslim slaves were among those owned by the Founding Fathers. For example, Spellberg found evidence suggesting that Muslim slaves owned by George Washington lived and labored on the Mount Vernon plantation.[8]

These early American Muslims faced many challenges in retaining a Muslim identity under the conditions of chattel slavery. The historian Michael Gomez explains that "Muslims would have had great difficulty in preserving Islam within their families."[9] Practices such as prayer, dietary restrictions, and veiling have been documented among West African slaves and their descendants in Georgia and South Carolina.[10] However, Muslim slaves did not have access to Islamic texts, and could not gather for communal prayer or other rituals. The conditions of slavery also meant that enslaved Muslims could be separated from their families at any time, making it difficult to pass on religious and cultural traditions to their children. Muslims were also a minority among the slave population (most slaves practiced other African religions and/or Christianity), meaning that often Muslims had little choice but to marry non-Muslims. During the nineteenth century there was also increased pressure to convert to Christianity.

Due to their race, the earliest American Muslims were excluded from the nation even as the founders determined that Muslims must, at least hypothetically, be granted freedom of religion and the opportunity to aspire to public office. When the Fourteenth Amendment was ratified in 1868, there were certainly practicing Muslims among the American-born former slaves who were granted citizenship.[11]

Due to the invisibility and suppression of Muslim identity and practice among West African slaves, the first Americans to be publicly recognized as Muslims were immigrants from the Middle East. These immigrants, many of them fleeing the crumbling Ottoman Empire, came primarily from what is now Jordan, Lebanon, Palestine, and Syria. Due to conventions at the time, these immigrants were often identified as "Syrian" despite their varied origins. Most of these immigrants were Christian, but a minority were Muslim. By and large, these immigrants were uneducated, and they found work in various unskilled professions: homesteaders and farmers in the Midwest, traveling peddlers (and later shopkeepers and merchants) in the cities, and manual laborers in factories. For example, the draw of the automobile industry in Detroit led to the concentration of Arabs and Muslims in nearby Dearborn, Michigan. Similarly, Toledo and Chicago saw concentrations of Muslim immigrants, as did Quincy, Massachusetts, where Lebanese Muslim immigrants gathered in the nineteenth century to work in the shipyards.[12] In Ross, North Dakota, immigrants from Syria began arriving in 1899. In 1929 the community was large enough to build what is believed to be the first purpose-built mosque in the United States.

Among these early immigrants was Hajji Ali, or as he was known in the United States, Hi Jolly. Hi Jolly stands out as a colorful historical figure and an early example of a Muslim in the U.S. military. Hi Jolly emigrated from Syria in 1856 and served in the U.S. Army for over thirty years as part of the short-lived Camel Corps. The Camel Corps was an experiment in using camels for freight transport in the Southwest where horses and mules struggled. In 1855, 33 camels (and 5 camel drivers) were brought to Texas. Ali was the main driver, and became known to the locals as Hi Jolly. The early expeditions with the camels (and Jolly) proved successful, and set the stage for the establishment of Army outposts throughout the Southwest. The Camel Corps fell out of use with the Civil War and eventually the remaining camels were sold or wandered off into the desert. Hi Jolly naturalized in 1880, married and had children, and later abandoned his family to prospect. He was denied a military pension despite his years of service, and he died destitute in 1902 in Quartzsite, Arizona. In 1934 the Arizona Highway Department replaced his wooden grave marker with a permanent memorial; that same year, the last surviving camel of the corps died and was buried with Jolly.[13]

The introduction of the "Asiatic Barred Zone" in 1917 and the subsequent introduction of national immigration quotas in 1921 and 1924 largely stopped the flow of Muslim immigrants into the United States. The Asiatic Barred Zone was legislation that prohibited immigration from Asia—an area defined to include South Asia and much of the Middle East. National quotas strongly favored immigrants from western Europe, particularly the United Kingdom, Ireland, and Germany. With access to their homelands largely cut off, and as a religious minority both in the United States and among their fellow immigrants, those Muslim immigrants already in the United States largely assimilated into the surrounding culture or formed communities based on shared ethnicity, rather than religion.[14]

During the period from the 1930s through the 1950s, white America was increasingly seeing Catholics and Jews as a part of the American mainstream, and the conceptualization of America as a Protestant nation needed to adapt. It is in this time period that the phrase *Judeo-Christian* gained popularity. While this idea was embraced as a way to combat anti-Jewish and anti-Catholic prejudices, it also continued to exclude Muslims, and "inadvertently became the basis for discrimination against Muslims in the twenty-first century."[15]

In 1965 immigration from the Islamic world resumed under the Hart-Celler Act. The new immigration legislation replaced national quotas with a system that gives priority to immigrants with family in the United States and to immigrants who have needed education and skills. Contemporary Muslim immigrants tend to be highly educated professionals.[16] Seeking opportunities for education, financial security, and safety from war and violence, when the gates to the United States reopened, Arabs, Iranians, and South Asians made up an unprecedented proportion of new immigrants.[17] Unlike previous generations of Muslim immigrants who came with few resources,

> the new arrivals had the financial resources and organizational skills they needed to pursue and perpetuate their faith. They opened mosques and Islamic centers, imported their prayer leaders and Koran readers from home, formed religious and Muslim professional associations, and generally set about re-creating much of the life they had left behind.[18]

Today it is estimated that Muslims comprise less than 1 percent of the total U.S. population. It is difficult to get an exact count of this population, but estimates range from about 3 million to 6 million.[19] American Muslims are racially and ethnically diverse. In fact, the Muslim community in the United States is the most ethnically and racially diverse such community in the world.[20] According to a 2011 publication by the Pew Research Center, of U.S. Muslims, 30 percent are white, 23 percent are black, 21 percent are Asian, 19 percent are other/mixed, and 6 percent are Hispanic. Pew also reported that 63 percent of the adult Muslim population in the United States is foreign-born, and 15 percent are the children of immigrants. Of foreign-born Muslims in the United States, 41 percent were born in the Middle East or North Africa, 26 percent in South Asia, 11 percent in Africa, 7 percent in Europe, 5 percent in Iran, and 10 percent elsewhere.[21]

ANTI-MUSLIM SENTIMENT IN THE CONTEMPORARY ERA

Through the centuries, negative ideas about Islam and Muslims began to form a coherent set of stereotypes that are clearly recognizable today. These themes developed great internal coherence in their representation of Muslims as an "other" in opposition to the West. Western images and understandings of Islam present it as monolithic, static, and antithetical to Western values.[22] Other themes include Muslims as primitive and uncivilized and Islam as evil or satanic.[23]

In the 1990s the political scientist Samuel Huntington introduced his controversial yet popular "clash of civilizations" theory, which has shaped the way these fears are articulated today. Huntington argued that current and future sources of conflict will largely be along the lines of competing "civilizations." In mapping these "civilizations" he categorized the world largely by religious tradition: Western, Confucian, Japanese, Islamic, Hindu, Slavic-Orthodox, Latin American, and African (order by Huntington). Huntington argued that the differences between civilizations are real and fundamental, and are "less mutable and hence less easily compromised and resolved than political and economic ones."[24] He argued that civilization ("What are you?") cannot be changed, suggesting that a Muslim literally cannot belong in the "West." Most research on Muslim American identification since 9/11 refutes this claim of incompatibility. Huntington also saw Islamic "civilization" as particularly dangerous, famously writing that "Islam has bloody borders."[25] Familiar themes of Islam as unchanging and threatening pervade his argument.

Among those who write and teach about Islam there are, broadly speaking, two camps. One side, exemplified by Karen Armstrong, presents a generally positive view of Islam and considers Islam to be a religion equivalent in scope and effect to other religions. At the other extreme are authors such as Daniel Pipes, who preach a doomsday scenario of an Islamic conspiracy to destroy the West. The latter camp often begin their discussion in terms of Islamism (a political movement), but quickly devolve into an association of all Muslims with fundamentalism, violence, and terrorism. This perspective takes the stance that Islam poses an existential threat; in his book *Militant Islam Reaches America*, Pipes writes, "The preservation of our existing order can no longer be taken for granted; it needs to be fought for."[26] The form of this threat is often proposed to be "creeping sharia," the idea that religious accommodation and multiculturalism will lead inexorably to a world in which "sharia law" (i.e., Islamic law) dictates the behavior of both Muslims and non-Muslims. This perspective is also marked by the belief that all Muslims are suspect, and that profiling is a justified and effective technique to combat terrorism. Pipes writes, "All Muslims, unfortunately are suspect."[27] Perhaps most troubling is the assertion from this camp that Muslims regularly practice *taqiyyah*, a form of deception believed by this camp to be pervasive.[28] This allows them to dismiss any Muslim who speaks against them on the assumption that they are lying.

The fear of Islam and Muslims is not new, nor are many of the forms it takes. The 9/11 attacks did not create these stereotypes, but they did reinvigorate a long-standing and often-latent sense of conflict and threat. 9/11 crystallized American fears of Islam and made many Americans feel vulnerable to an Islamic threat.[29]

MUSLIM AMERICANS AND THE "WAR ON TERRORISM"

9/11 acted as a spark which reignited ancient stereotypes that claimed that Islam and the West were mutually exclusive and in perpetual conflict. Following the attacks, media coverage often relied on the familiar stereotypes. In this time of uncertainty, perhaps there was even some comfort in the familiarity of these stereotypes. Complex events were simplified into a story of "us-versus-them," and a dominant narrative emerged that explained the events as a result of "them" being fundamentally different from "us."[30] Stereotypes of Muslims as backward, primitive, and tyrannical were used to explain how it was Muslims' incompatibility with "our" democracy and freedom that led to the attacks. On September 20, 2001, President George W. Bush summed up this narrative in his famed statement, "You are either with us, or you are with the terrorists."

In the same speech, President Bush did rhetorically draw a distinction between the religion of Islam and terrorism: "The enemy of America is not our many Muslim friends; it is not our many Arab friends. Our enemy is a radical network of terrorists, and every government that supports them."[31] Although the official rhetoric framed the enemy in vague terms as "terrorists," the actions that were being taken by the government could be seen as targeting specific populations; populations that centuries of stereotypes had prepared Americans to see as dangerous. Policies requiring the registration of men from countries as diverse as Oman and Somalia,[32] the detention of over a thousand Muslims, monitoring of mosques by the FBI, and watch lists full of Muslim names provided a clear picture of who the enemy was. Geographically, racially, and culturally different groups were all primarily identifiable by a shared label: Muslim. The invasion of Afghanistan and Iraq, predominantly Muslim countries, meant that images of Muslim enemies pervaded the media. The writer Moustafa Bayoumi commented that "the actions of [the Bush] administration spoke louder than his words."[33]

In 2011 and 2012 Representative Peter King, chair of the Committee on Homeland Security, held several investigative hearings on the radicalization of American Muslims and aimed "to examine the threat of violent radicalization emanating from within the Muslim-American community."[34] The report on the fifth hearing (the topic of which was "The American Muslim Response to Hearings on Radicalization within Their Community") claims that the hearings offered "irrefutable proof of the extent of the radicalization threat." The narrative surrounding these hearings paralleled those used to justify the NYPD's surveillance program and federal registration policies. This narrative frames Muslims as inherently dangerous. Bayoumi describes this narrative as it relates to the NYPD surveillance program: "The reasoning behind their actions must be their belief that Muslims will almost necessarily become, it they aren't already, terrorists or supporters of terrorism."[35]

Scholars who study war are familiar with the ways in which groups associated with the enemy are dehumanized. For example, the historian John Dower described the portrayal of the Japanese in American culture during World War II and found that they were commonly depicted as primitives, children, and madmen. Dower argued that these same ways of thinking were attached to new enemies as they arose, including the Soviets, Chinese, Koreans, and Vietnamese.[36] It is easy to identify these same trends in media coverage of the "War on Terror." The sociologist Jeffrey Alexander describes the way war tends to create a perception of good ("us") versus evil ("them"). The group associated with "them" comes to be seen as the opposite of "us."[37] This narrative was ready to be set in motion when it came to Islam; it was a part of what Edward Said refers to as the "subliminal cultural consciousness" about Islam,[38] and it easily became a part of the narrative around the "War on Terror." To engage in killing, the enemy must be seen as so intractable that only violent action is appropriate: "it becomes impossible for good people to treat and reason with those on the other side. If one's opponents are beyond reason [. . .] the only option is to read them out of the human race."[39]

The ability to dehumanize Muslims as enemies during the "War on Terror" can be seen in a variety of military practices and the general lack of civilian outrage against these. There is, for example, the use of drones to carry out assassinations that have been characterized as "erasing" America's enemies.[40] Based on reporting by the *New York Times* and *The Nation*, Bayoumi described a system in which the label "potential terrorist" is imputed to as many causalities of drone strikes as possible in an effort to obscure the number of civilian casualties.[41] Official guidance from the White House explicitly denies this.[42] Other practices such as "enhanced interrogation techniques," Guantanamo Prison and the policy of indefinite detention, the "rendition" program, as well as the scandal at Abu Ghraib prison in Iraq are cases that are associated with Muslim enemies who are viewed as so unlike "us" that the extrajudicial and extreme methods used against them no longer seem shocking to the American public. When Muslims outside the United States are regularly dehumanized in these ways, it is not surprising to find violence against Muslims in the United States increase.

FBI hate crime statistics show a dramatic increase in anti-Islamic hate crimes in 2001, from about 30 incidents per year in the late 1990s to a high of 481 in 2001. Hate crimes have declined since then, but they remain about three times what they were prior to 9/11. The Council on American-Islamic Relations (CAIR) issues annual Civil Rights Reports which also show evidence of anti-Islamic prejudice. Cases documented by CAIR include vandalism of mosques, arson, beatings, and murder.

ISLAMOPHOBIA

The reinvigoration of anti-Muslim stereotypes following 9/11 posed Muslims as the "other" and the enemy and therefore acceptable targets for various social penalties. Studies of Muslim youth following 9/11 provide a window into life as a Muslim American. The sociologist Lori Peek interviewed Muslim college and university students in New York City following 9/11. Her respondents reported negative responses ranging "from stares and 'nasty looks' to verbal harassment and even physical assault."[43]

The anthropologists Katherine Pratt Ewing and Marguerite Hoyler found similar patterns in their study of South Asian Muslim youths in North Carolina. Their respondents reported feelings of marginalization and that their identities as Americans and Muslims had been politicized. Ewing and Hoyler noted that the atmosphere following 9/11 and the discourse surrounding the wars in Afghanistan and Iraq "deprived most of the youth we met of a sense of full cultural citizenship as Muslims came to be positioned more explicitly as outsiders."[44] A respondent from Peek's study echoes this sentiment: "When they say 'America Unites,' they did not mean us. They did not mean Muslims. At every moment when they said, 'America must unite,' they did not mean us."[45]

Both studies noted that even though physical violence was rare, the knowledge that such violence existed shaped feelings of exclusion. "The message of the anti-Muslim violence seemed clear: Muslims are not 'real' Americans. [. . .] To many young Muslims, anti-Muslim violence conveyed the message that they could not be both Muslim and American and that they would never be considered as such."[46] In addition to violence, policies such as increased scrutiny at airports were experienced as a form of symbolic violence. Even when experienced only at secondhand, the perceived humiliation and ill-treatment of family and community members shaped the perceptions of these young people. Being a victim of harassment or violence personally was not necessary to feel excluded, othered, and frightened.[47]

Selcuk Sirin and Michelle Fine, in their study of identity formation, found similar patterns. "One of the most disturbing findings from our studies of Muslim youth over the past five years was the degree to which they have absorbed discriminatory acts into their lives."[48] They reported that these adolescents "described being watched, talked about, or suspected in public spaces, on the subway, at school, at home, and in their neighborhoods."[49] They also noted the ways in which this surveillance and judgment was gendered:

> The young Muslim men walked in the shadow of the label of *terrorist* and heard comments like "They hate women"; "They hate Christians"; and "They are really violent." Young Muslim women, in contrast, walked in the shadow of the label *oppressed*.[50]

In the current context it is often assumed that it is easy to tell if someone is Muslim (and therefore subject to the stereotypes) by how they look. One way this works is the assumption that Muslims share a "brown" phenotype. Several of the people who spoke with me did identify themselves as "brown." "Brown" is a racial identity used by many groups, including South Asians, Arabs, Hispanics, and others who do not fit well into the black/white ideas of race common in the United States. The term *brown* is used by some and rejected by others. It is not a label embraced by all Arabs and South Asians, but it is a concept that is generally understood to capture the distinct experience of being what the sociologist Nazli Kibria terms "ambiguous non-whites."[51] Since 9/11, being Muslim has become associated with being "brown" and being "brown" has become associated with being Muslim. The attorney Sunita Patel argues that "following September 11, mainstream media, perpetrators of hate violence and speech, and many activists began thinking of 'Muslim-looking' Arabs, Muslims, and South Asians as a single racial group."[52] This is a problematic assumption. Because there are Muslims of many different races, the stereotype of Muslims as "brown" is an oversimplification that associates being Muslim with being Arab or South Asian, though not all Arabs or South Asians would necessarily be labeled as "brown" based on their appearance. It is an assumption that fails on many different levels.

Another common assumption is that Muslims (and only Muslims) dress a certain way. Attire associated with being Muslim includes the *hijab*—a headscarf—and the long robe known as an *abaya* or *jilbab* for women. For men, attire includes a beard, a skullcap, commonly called a *kufi*, and clothes such as a *thobe*—a long robe common in the Arabian Gulf—or *shalwar khameez*, an outfit consisting of pants and a long tunic common in South Asia.[53] Muslims may or may not wear any of these items of clothing, and decisions about how to dress are complicated by the recognition that clothing choice may be perceived by others through a lens of anti-Muslim stereotypes.

The idea that there is a specific Muslim look is problematic because it connects appearance with negative stereotypes about Muslims. As a result, a particular appearance—whether complexion or attire—can elicit negative responses. The social scientist Nasar Meer notes that in the United Kingdom "many British Muslims report a higher level of discrimination and abuse when they appear 'conspicuously Muslim.'"[54] This issue gained attention in the United States when Juan Williams, an analyst for National Public Radio, made the comment, "But when I get on the plane, I got to tell you, if I see people who are in Muslim garb and I think, you know, they are identifying themselves first and foremost as Muslims, I get worried. I get nervous."[55] The focus on appearance can lead to misidentification, and when combined with tendencies toward violence, can have tragic results, as in the fatal shooting of Balbir Singh Sodhi on September 15, 2001. An Indian Sikh, Sodhi was mistaken for a Muslim and killed by a man seeking to retaliate for 9/11 by killing Muslims. In August 2012 a white supremacist attacked a Sikh temple in Oak Creek, Wisconsin, killing six people (and himself). As of this writing, the FBI, which has taken jurisdiction of the case, has not issued any statements about the motives for the attack. Many have speculated that mistaken religion played a role. Bayoumi describes this line of thinking and the problems inherent in the reporting on these cases of "mistaken identity":

> It's true we don't know Page's precise motivations, but in all likelihood it wasn't Sikhophobia, a term barely known in the United States. It was Islamophobia. That's why to say that Page made a "mistake" in targeting Sikhs, as many have reported, or that Sikhs are "unfairly" targeted as Muslims [. . .] is to imply that it would be "correct" to attack Muslims.[56]

Although it is now fifteen years after 9/11, the fear and hatred that was catalyzed by these attacks remains prevalent in American society. The uncertainty felt by some people at the changing demographics of the United States combined with savage terrorist attacks at home and abroad has led to a surge in anti-Muslim narratives. The content of these narratives reflects the history of anti-Muslim ideas in the United States.

Although Barack Obama is the first black president of the United States, he is not the first presidential candidate to be accused by political rivals of being a Muslim in an attempt to undermine him. In the election of 1800, John Adams's campaign accused Thomas Jefferson of being a Muslim. The historian Denise Spellberg explains:

> The accusation that Jefferson was a Muslim placed him, unknowingly, in the same category as his intellectual hero John Locke, who was charged with professing "the faith of a Turk," and even George Sale, the British translator of his Qur'an, [was] derided as "half a Musselman." These three (and others before them) became [. . .] victims of long-standing tradition of anti-Islamic defamation.[57]

In December 2015, during his presidential campaign, Donald Trump issued a statement calling for "a total and complete shutdown of Muslims entering the United States." He characterized Muslims as having "hatred [. . .] beyond comprehension," and having "no sense of reason or respect for human life."[58] These characterizations are familiar and repeat claims made against Muslims immediately following 9/11, but also for centuries before that. Donald Trump has recently been elected president. At this time, it is unclear what effects, if any, the rhetoric of the campaign trail will have on his policies.

In July 2016, former House speaker Newt Gingrich drew on familiar themes in expressing his desire to impose religious tests on Muslims. In an interview he stated, "Western civilization is in a war. We should frankly test every person here who is of Muslim background and if they believe in sharia, they should be deported. Sharia is incompatible with Western civilization." Familiar themes here include characterizing "Western civilization" and Islam as separate and incompatible entities, framing Islam and Muslims as an existential threat, and perpetuating fears of "creeping sharia" while handily demonstrating ignorance of the theological complexity of this concept. Even the calls for a religious test are passé; this notion was rigorously debated in the 1780s and the decision to reject such tests as un-American was enshrined in Article 6 of the Constitution.

Fortunately, seeing Muslims as a threatening "them" was not the only way in which American society reacted to 9/11. While there were expressions of anger and violence against Muslims, there were also outpourings of support, friendship, and dialogue. Reality is complex, and it is grossly oversimplifying matters to suggest that there was only one way in which Muslims and non-Muslims interacted following 9/11. What I am arguing is that negative views of Islam and Muslims were ascendant. In attempting to deal with a complex conflict centered in a region of the world unfamiliar to many Americans, involving individuals of a faith with which most Americans had no personal contact, it was easy to use existing stereotypes that claimed "they" are fundamentally different and therefore incompatible with "our" society. This became what social scientists call the "dominant discourse." While there are many stories that we could be sharing about Muslims in the United States, the most prevalent ones that we do hear are ones that support this idea that Muslims and Islam are "always and forever a foreign and a foreigner's faith to the United States."[59] In this book, I seek to tell stories that add complexity to this troubling dominant discourse.

MUSLIM AMERICAN IDENTITY

What, then, does it mean to be Muslim American after 9/11? The dominant narratives in the culture claim that Americans and Muslims are mutually exclusive categories and that Muslims are backward, dangerous, and a violent threat to Americans. Muslim Americans encounter this narrative throughout society. Television shows like *Homeland* and *24* rely on motifs of Muslims as untrustworthy, dangerous, and deserving of torture.[60] Movies like *American Sniper* have been criticized for their depictions of Arabs and Muslims as monolithic, evil, and less than human.[61] Interactions between Muslims and law enforcement may be shaped by the history of surveillance, while their community interactions at the mosque, fund-raisers, or just in general are shaped by knowledge of the government tactic of using informants and undercover operatives.[62] At the university, students study theories that claim that "Muslim American" is an impossible identity. Political races from local elections to the presidential race include candidates and pundits calling for law enforcement to "patrol and secure Muslim neighborhoods,"[63] ban Muslims from entering the country, and test Muslims about their religious beliefs and deport those who do not "pass" this test. Meanwhile, dressing in particular ways may invite stares, comments, and in rare (but unpredictable) cases, violence. Going to worship becomes a fraught experience when mosques in recent years have been vandalized, set on fire, shot at, and even targeted with homemade explosives.[64] In 2015 a man was verbally and physically attacked after praying in a public park.[65] During Ramadan in 2016 there were several violent attacks against worshippers, including a man who was beaten in Florida and a man shot in Texas.[66] Almost everywhere you turn, you encounter the message that "Muslim" and "American" do not go together. This idea can even be found reproduced in publications seeking to demonstrate the integration of American Muslims. The Pew Research Center in its 2011 report on Muslim Americans asked respondents whether they think of themselves first as an American or as a Muslim. This question forces the respondent to pick one identity over the other in a way that does not represent the experiences of many American Muslims.[67]

It is assumed that Muslim Americans must choose whether they are American or Muslim. Despite this assumption and the pressure to prioritize identities, for many American Muslims, there is nothing to choose between because the identities of Muslim and American are not experienced as being in opposition.

Selcuk Sirin and Michelle Fine explored the processes of identity negotiation among immigrant Muslim youths in the United States following 9/11. They found that for most of the Muslim youths they worked with, Muslim and American are compatible identities:

> Contrary to what many have predicted, Muslims in this country have not "given up" their American identity for the sake of their Muslim identity, despite the many pressures from Muslim fundamentalists and some Western intellectuals, who claim that one cannot be a good American and a good Muslim at the same time.[68]

SUMMARY

Within this context, thousands of Muslims have chosen to join the U.S. military. Many served on the front lines and some died while serving. Military service is only one of many ways that Muslim Americans demonstrate their own sense of integration in the face of the stereotypes and assumptions described above. The dominant narrative can make it difficult to hear these stories that complicate the idea that the world is simply "us" and "them." In addition to the importance of these stories as examples of the complexity of real life, the setting of the U.S. military is a fascinating one for exploring questions of belonging and Americanness. In chapter 2, I will explain why the military is a useful place to look at issues of diversity and integration.

TWO

THE MILITARY CONTEXT

During the nineteenth and early twentieth centuries, military forces in the United States and Europe were large in size, at least during wartime, and were often referred to as "mass armies." Usually these military forces relied on conscription to fill the ranks and their primary mission involved large-scale combat. With the end of World War II, many nations, including the United States, started to reduce the size of their active forces. Though the Cold War meant troop levels remained relatively high, the specter of nuclear warfare meant there was less emphasis on sheer numbers of troops and more emphasis on technology. Following the end of the Cold War, the U.S. military downsized, and missions began to shift away from war-fighting to what are referred to as "military operations other than war" (MOOTW). MOOTW tasks include peacekeeping and humanitarian missions. However, after 9/11, the U.S. military once again became a war-fighting force with troops on the ground in both Afghanistan and Iraq. U.S. troops entered Afghanistan in 2001 in pursuit of the terrorist group al-Qaeda. In March 2003 U.S. troops invaded Iraq.

Although less than 1 percent of the American population serves in the military, the military is a social institution that plays a prominent role in American society. From video games[1] to music videos[2] to yellow-ribbon car magnets,[3] the military is deeply embedded in everyday life. The military both symbolically and practically represents the United States, both at home and abroad. As such, it is an excellent place to consider questions of belonging and inclusion. Understanding the experiences of minorities in the military is important to understanding what is happening in American society. In addition to serving a central practical and symbolic role in the nation, the U.S. military is an institution with an interesting history regarding diversity.

A BRIEF OVERVIEW OF DIVERSITY IN THE MILITARY

The military has had varied experiences when it comes to diversity in the ranks. The U.S. military was ahead of civilian society in racial integration. In civilian society, the landmark integration decision in *Brown v. Board of Education* was handed down by the Supreme Court in 1954. Prior to this, in 1948, President Harry Truman issued Executive Order 9981 ordering the military to revisit its racial policies in order to assure "equality of treatment and opportunity for all persons in the armed services without regard to race, color, religion or national origin."[4] In effect this set the stage for the integration of blacks and whites in the U.S. military. In 1951, following the onset of the Korean War, the military began to desegregate units. The last all-black unit was abolished in 1954, the same year *Brown v. Board of Education* enshrined principles of integration in the civilian world. Those who study the military often comment on the swiftness of this change, arguing that the military was able to effectively make such dramatic changes ahead of civilian society because of unique characteristics of the military, such as its hierarchical structure. On the other hand, the integration of women and LGBT individuals in the U.S. military has been much slower. While the military led civilian society in racial integration, it has lagged behind in gender and sexuality integration.

The military is a practical organization, and diversity policies vary as the needs of the organization change. One of the driving factors for increasing diversity in the military is the need for personnel. From the earliest days of American military history, need has trumped other concerns. Although George Washington halted the recruitment of black soldiers in 1775, the loss of large numbers of soldiers to disease and desertion led him to accept black soldiers into the Continental Army by 1778.[5] More recently, the end of conscription in 1973 led to dramatic personnel shortfalls. As the military faced low recruitment numbers without the ability to compel service, new policies were put in place to encourage minorities to take on jobs that white men were no longer filling in the required numbers.[6]

RACIAL INTEGRATION IN THE U.S. MILITARY

Although blacks have served in every U.S. conflict, their roles have often been contested and debated. In World War I, black men[7] were allowed to serve in segregated, all-black units. While a few of these units served in combat, many served in support roles, working as butchers, stevedores, and manual laborers. In World War II, a policy of strict racial segregation remained. A 1940 Army statement explained:

> The policy of the War Department is not to intermingle colored and white enlisted personnel in the same regimental organizations. The policy has been proven satisfactory over a long period of years and to make changes would produce situations destructive to morale and detrimental to the preparations for national defense.[8]

Personnel needs did mean that blacks were allowed to serve in all-black platoons within white companies. For example, 2,500 black soldiers fought during the Battle of the Bulge (1944–45) in these platoons. The all-black Tuskegee Airmen were another example of the strict adherence to racial segregation. Black women also served. For example, the sociologist Brenda Moore documents the experiences of the only black women's unit to serve overseas.[9] Black service members made up about 10 percent of military personnel during the war, and despite some units in combat, most remained in support positions.[10] By the end of World War II, discussions about integration were underway.[11]

During the Korean War, the Operations Research Office surveyed soldiers about issues relating to segregation and desegregation of military units. The project, code-named "Clear," found that integrated units were equally or more effective than segregated ones. Project Clear and subsequent studies argued that racial integration would increase military effectiveness and recommended an end to segregation. By the Vietnam War, all branches of the U.S. armed forces were racially integrated.

With the end of conscription in 1973, the proportion of minorities in the U.S. military increased. As white men opted out of the now-voluntary service, military officials worked to create more enticing working conditions, ultimately attracting many minorities who felt the military offered them more opportunity than the civilian labor force. This shifted military race relations policy toward a focus on equality of opportunity. The effects of these policies can be seen in the dramatic increase of minority service members. Racial and ethnic minorities account for about 30 percent of active duty service members, with black service members composing 16 percent of the military.[12]

Although the military is far from perfect when it comes to race relations,[13] a consistent pattern found by those who study race in the military is that conditions are often better in the military than in civilian society.[14] The military sociologist Charles Moskos sums up this sentiment: "in the Army blacks see more racial discrimination than whites, but differences in perception are much smaller in the Army than in civilian life."[15]

JAPANESE AMERICANS IN WORLD WAR II

Japanese Americans successfully used military service in World War II to renegotiate their position in society from suspected enemy to model minority. Early in the war, they faced extremely negative policies. However, exemplary military service and sacrifice were used to successfully incorporate them into the nation.

Because Japanese Americans were already seen as a threat because of the economic challenge they posed to the white population, with the onset of the war, the dominant narrative about Japanese Americans worsened. Japanese Americans were stigmatized for belonging to the same ethnicity as the enemy. They became targets for the desire for revenge and fears during early Japanese victories in the war, and "the Nisei[16] were now being socially constructed as belonging to another human species, incapable of being loyal citizens of the United States."[17] In response many Nisei emphasized their American citizenship.

On February 19, 1942, President Franklin Roosevelt signed Executive Order 9066, which granted the War Department control of "enemy aliens" and the distinction between citizen and alien lost meaning.[18] Japanese Americans on the West Coast were evacuated from their homes and interned in camps. Japanese Americans in Hawaii did not face mass evacuation although representatives of the Japanese government, Shinto and Buddhist priests and priestesses, language teachers, and fishermen were detained.[19] Following the attack on Pearl Harbor in 1941, there was no immediate policy regarding Japanese American soldiers, and commanding officers acted on their own discretion; while some Nisei were allowed to continue with their regular duties, many were disarmed, reassigned, transferred, or discharged.[20]

In June 1942 the War Department and Selective Service System reclassified all Nisei as 4-C, "aliens ineligible for military service," and stopped their induction.[21] Then, in January 1943, the War Department announced it was seeking volunteers for the formation of a special combat team[22] of Japanese Americans which came to be known as the 442nd Regimental Combat Team. At the time, the military was segregated into white and black units; fitting poorly into this dichotomy, Japanese American soldiers could have been integrated into existing units (and some did serve as interpreters and in intelligence positions in white combat units). But the creation of an all-Nisei unit was seen by the U.S. Army as a means by which Japanese Americans could demonstrate their loyalty. Part of the rationale for forming a segregated unit was that a separate unit's performance would be noticed and could serve to refute the charges of disloyalty, while the service of individual Nisei scattered throughout the Army would be more difficult to measure.[23] Members of the unit made deliberate efforts to present themselves favorably, including close attention to their uniform, meticulous adherence to military courtesy, eschewing the use of Japanese, regular and repeated blood donations, and buying war bonds. Mike Masaoka worked during the war as a publicist for the 442nd, interviewing Nisei soldiers and sending stories back for distribution in United States. He reported:

> In all I wrote more than 2,000 stories, with many of the interviews being conducted under combat conditions. "Why are you out here fighting for your country?" I would ask these men. In other outfits the reply might be a wisecrack, like "The draft board got me before I could get away." With the Nisei the invariable answer was: "Because we want to prove ourselves as Americans."[24]

In April 1943 Nisei women were officially allowed to volunteer for the Women's Army Corps (WAC).[25] They were not racially segregated. Moore found that the Nisei women volunteering for WAC service "felt a great need to show loyalty to the United States" and joined the military to prove they were Americans.[26] She identified the treatment of Japanese Americans as a driving force, inspiring "super-patriotism" among the Nisei. Some of Moore's respondents identified the military service of Nisei as instrumental in the establishment of full citizenship rights for Japanese Americans, and most saw it as contributing to personal upward social mobility. The recruitment of Nisei women drew explicitly on the connection between military service and citizenship; for example, one recruiting press release read:

> All Americans, whatever their ancestry, must remember that they will be judged in the future by the part they play now. If we shirk our plain duty to our country in a time of its greatest need, we must be prepared to have our loyalty questioned. Indeed, I think it should be questioned.[27]

According to Masaoka, reestablishing the draft for Nisei men was seen as crucial to the claiming of citizenship rights for Japanese Americans. In a speech to the Japanese American Citizens League he proclaimed:

> Let me ask you to think of your future—and that of your children's children. When the war is won, and we attempt to find our way back into normal society, one question which we cannot avoid will be, "Say, Buddy, what did you do in the war?" If we cannot answer that we, with them, fought for the victory which is ours, our chance for success and acceptance will be small. We need Selective Service, the least we can do is to ask for it. [. . .] I call for a resolution to the President and the Army of the United States asking for a reclassification of the draft status of the American-born Japanese so that we shall be accorded the same privilege of serving our country in the armed forces as that granted to every other American citizen.[28]

In January 1944 the War Department reinstated the draft of Japanese American men and classified them as 1-A, "immediately eligible for conscription."[29] The all-Nisei units served admirably in the war and received favorable media coverage. The all-Nisei units received many military awards, including 9,486 Purple Hearts.[30] As the Nisei units demonstrated their dedication in fighting overseas, the media was eager to follow their exploits. By 1945 Japanese American families in the United States were greeted by white neighbors with inquiries about "your boys in Italy," and employment and housing became notably easier to obtain.[31] The sociologist Tamotsu Shibutani argued that the unexpected achievements of the units were the impetus for the stereotype of Japanese Americans as an overachieving, model minority group.

For Japanese Americans during World War II, military service was used to directly claim citizenship. Since the Nisei were initially excluded from conscription, military service itself was a form of citizenship they had to fight for. The military service of a select group of Japanese Americans became an important stepping-stone by which the entire community made claims of national belonging.

GENDER DIVERSITY IN THE U.S. MILITARY

Women's military roles have changed slowly over the years, reflecting both social changes and military needs.[32] In 1917, during World War I, the U.S. Navy established women's units, and the Marine Corps followed suit in 1918. These women wore military uniforms and performed tasks as telephone operators and clerks; some were stationed overseas. Women's military roles reflected the roles of women in civilian society.[33]

World War II saw an expansion of women's roles. As with racially segregated units, women served in gender-segregated units. These women primarily worked in traditionally feminine fields such as nursing, and as clerks, typists, and switchboard operators, but a small number served in traditionally more masculine fields, working as airplane mechanics, parachute riggers, and weapons instructors.[34]

The service of these women led to the 1948 Women's Armed Services Integration Act, which officially created a permanent place for women in the U.S. military, though women's roles were tightly constrained. Under this act, women could constitute no more than 2 percent of the force, they could not be permanently promoted above the rank of lieutenant colonel/commander, and they were barred from service aboard Navy vessels (with the exception of hospital ships and transports) and from service on aircraft on combat missions. In 1967 Congress removed the 2 percent ceiling and the limits on women's promotion.[35]

As with racial diversity, the end of conscription in 1973 is crucial to understanding subsequent changes in gender diversity in the military. The end of conscription and resulting personnel shortfalls led the military to open additional roles to racial minorities and to women,[36] leading to a dramatic increase in the number of women serving in the military.[37] Women began serving as aviators, and in 1976 Congress opened the service academies to women.[38]

By the 2000s, 80 percent of active component positions were open to women, with prohibitions only on their service on submarines and in offensive ground combat positions. Despite formal limitations on their service in offensive combat, women were involved in combat in Afghanistan and Iraq.[39] Based in part on this performance, in January 2013 the Department of Defense officially rescinded the direct combat exclusion. As of 2016, each service branch has begun implementing plans to fully integrate women.

SEXUAL ORIENTATION DIVERSITY IN THE U.S. MILITARY

As with other marginalized groups, gay men and lesbians have served throughout the history of the U.S. military. Some contributions continue to shape the U.S. military; for example, Friedrich von Steuben, an openly gay Prussian officer, developed what came to be known as the American Army's Doctrine on Drill and Ceremony.[40]

Since World War II, the U.S. military maintained policies prohibiting homosexuals from serving in the military. Formalized in 1982, the Department of Defense (DoD) policy stated that "homosexuality is incompatible with military service," citing, among other things, the believed adverse effects of homosexuals on discipline, order, and morale.[41] President William "Bill" Clinton was responding to this policy when, in the early 1990s, he called for congressional hearings on lifting this ban. This process led to a compromise in the form of the policy Don't Ask, Don't Tell (DADT), enacted in 1994. Under DADT, gay men and lesbians would be allowed to serve so long as their sexual orientation was kept secret.

The beginning of the "War on Terror" in 2001 and the concomitant need for personnel seems to have led to a deemphasis on enforcing DADT as the number of service members discharged under DADT decreased dramatically. As psychologist Bonnie Moradi and social scientist Laura Miller observe, "reduced enforcement of the policy during wartime calls into question whether military commanders agree with the policy that the impact of lesbian and gay service members outweighs the contributions those service members make to their units' mission."[42] By 2008, 75 percent of Americans favored repealing the policy.[43] In September 2011 DADT was ended. Public pressure and work by LGBT rights advocates played an important role in the repeal of DADT.

MILITARY STRUCTURE AND DIVERSITY

Some characteristics that have helped the military quickly integrate new groups include the hierarchical structure of the military. In many ways, racial integration of the military was successful because it occurred under specific military conditions. Moore argues that what makes the military remarkable "is not its policy of racial equality, which is found in every institution in the United States, but its ability, through its organizational structure, to enforce this policy."[44]

Racial integration began under conditions of conscription, and rapid integration was possible because the military was already in the business of coercing service members from diverse backgrounds to work and live together. The authoritarian nature of military service and the emphasis on hierarchy also allowed the military to enforce behavioral change and compliance.

Leo Bogart, one of the authors of Project Clear, the Korean War–era research project on desegregation, also felt that it was important that service members were separated from civilian society during their service, facilitating rapid integration. At the time Bogart was investigating integration, the Army was a "closed society"; soldiers experiencing the changing policies were separated from social networks at home and did not have to take into account the expectations, opinions, or pressures of family, friends, and neighbors in interacting with diverse colleagues.[45]

The U.S. military has also officially embraced policies of equal opportunity (EO) and many aspects of military life emphasize this. For example, in the Army there are two formal positions that support EO policies. At the brigade level,[46] each command has a full-time equal opportunity advisor (EOA) who is responsible for advising the command on EO issues as well as monitoring EO issues and complaints and organizing events to promote diversity. EOAs receive education and training at the Defense Equal Opportunity Management Institute (DEOMI), where they undergo two and a half months of study. At the company level, part-time equal opportunity representatives (EOR) advise and assist commanders in carrying out their EO duties. EORs provide support but do not process complaints.[47]

In addition to formal policies explicitly addressing equality of opportunity, other aspects of the military organization may help facilitate integration. Moskos identified aspects of military service, such as pay by rank, uniformity of dress, code of discipline, common duties, shared facilities, and even title ("soldier") as factors which neutralize differences among service members. The military also instills a shared worldview and a common military culture in its members. This can create a sense of a military "in-group" that overrides individual differences.[48]

While there are aspects of military service that have the potential to increase inclusion, it is important to point out that the military is also an institution that practices closure and exclusion both formally and informally. For example, the military has historically been, and remains, a masculine institution. The military is a unique social institution in that until recently it could legally disqualify applicants from certain jobs based solely on gender and sexual orientation.

THE CONTACT HYPOTHESIS AND THE MILITARY

Upon considering the racial integration of the U.S. military, the psychologist Gordon Allport formulated a theory now referred to as the "contact hypothesis."[49] Central in many studies of diversity, the contact hypothesis argues that contact between individuals with different backgrounds is a means of breaking down prejudice. Since prejudice and group conflict are often based on stereotyping, the opportunity to communicate with members of another group can lead to greater appreciation and understanding of alternative perspectives and experiences, and thereby diminish prejudice.

Allport argued that contact alone is not enough, and that certain conditions must be met to transform interactions into acceptance. Casual contact—passing on the street or in the store, for example—does not break down stereotypes, but may instead strengthen them if adverse stereotypes are reinforced. On the other hand, in-depth contact under certain conditions has the potential to lessen prejudice. This can be achieved through education, but direct experience is better. "Contacts that bring knowledge and acquaintance are likely to engender sounder beliefs concerning minority groups, and for this reason contribute to the reduction of prejudice."[50] The "other" comes to be seen as a complex human being through in-depth contact; prejudices based on simplistic and inaccurate conceptualizations break down. Being around people different than you is a start, but it is not enough according to Allport, who argued, "The nub of the matter seems to be the contact must reach below the surface in order to be effective in altering prejudice. Only the type of contact that leads people to *do* things together is likely to result in changed attitudes."[51]

In order to break down prejudice, contact must be meaningful contact, not just diversity for the sake of diversity; additionally, contact must occur between individuals of similar status and preferably with institutional support:

> Prejudice (unless deeply rooted in the character structure of the individual) may be reduced by equal status contact between majority and minority groups in the pursuit of common goals. The effect is greatly enhanced if this contact is sanctioned by institutional supports (i.e., by law, custom or local atmosphere), and provided it is of a sort that leads to the perception of common interests and common humanity between members of the two groups.[52]

These criteria are met in the military, where service members often work in diverse groups toward shared goals, and where regulations officially promote integration.

The role of intergroup contact is also clear in the findings of Project Clear. In this study, both white and black soldiers who had served in integrated units were much more favorable toward the idea of integration than were those who had served in only segregated units. One of the principal findings was that attitudes toward integration were shaped by experiences serving in integrated units:

Men learn to accept integration. As it is experienced, attitudes become more favorable. Thus the probable success of any new attempt at integration may be gauged not in terms of what attitudes men hold at present, but in terms of what attitudes they are likely to hold under the impact of their new experience.[53]

MUSLIMS IN THE U.S. MILITARY

Muslims serve throughout the U.S. armed forces. Estimates of the number of Muslims in the U.S. military vary widely; reports range from a low of 3,400[54] to a high of 15,000.[55] The Defense Manpower Data Center (DMDC) collects official data on religious affiliation, and as of March 2009, reported a total of 3,535 Muslims serving in the active forces and 1,503 in the reserves. These are the estimates commonly used by the media; however, these data have some significant limitations. The DMDC collects these data voluntarily upon entry into the military, and so cannot account for individuals who choose not to reveal their religion, those who change their religion during their service, or the degree of religiosity of service members.

Muslims serve in enlisted and officer roles across the United States and the globe. They have studied at all of the military academies: the Military Academy at West Point, the Naval Academy in Annapolis, and the Air Force Academy in Colorado Springs. Many have served in combat and support positions throughout the conflicts in Afghanistan and Iraq. Some have been wounded or killed in these conflicts.[56] According to a Congressional Research Services Report on diversity in the armed forces, Muslims comprised approximately 0.3 percent of the active duty force in January 2015.[57] This is a slight underrepresentation given that Muslims are estimated to be approximately 1 percent of the total U.S. population.

Muslim chaplains were first commissioned in the 1990s,[58] and all the branches of the military currently have Muslim chaplains. In order to be commissioned as a chaplain, a candidate must pass required educational and physical standards set by the military as well as be supported by a recognized endorsing organization of his or her religion. For religious groups like Muslims, Buddhists, and pagans, who do not have a unified hierarchical structure in the United States, this last requirement poses the biggest hurdle to commissioning chaplains.

Even though they are few and far between, the existence of Muslim chaplains is important. Kim Hansen identified minority chaplains as important for inclusion.[59] Most of the people who spoke with me did not have substantial interactions with

Muslim chaplains. More common was interaction with lay leaders. Lay leaders are service members who volunteer to provide some religious services. Lay leaders are not clergy and must be approved by the military (and in some cases also by their religious group). In the Muslim context, a lay leader might provide support such as leading prayers since this can be done by any person meeting some basic requirements of knowledge. Muslims may seek out a recognized religious leader, generally called an "imam," for spiritual advice and guidance, for religious education, or to officiate at rituals such as marriages, funerals, or conversions. These are roles a Muslim chaplain, or perhaps a lay leader, would be able to fulfill. In other cases, service members are able to seek religious support in the local civilian community. Muslim service members can also seek support from non-Muslim chaplains. Military chaplains provide support to all service members regardless of faith. The support a non-Muslim chaplain could provide includes general counseling, assisting a service member in requesting formal religious accommodation, ordering specific products, such as religiously appropriate Meals Ready to Eat (MREs), and providing education and advice to leadership about the diverse religious needs of members of the unit.

Military service members give up some of the rights of civilian society, such as the right to trial by jury; however, the right to free exercise of religion is protected, and with a few exceptions, military service members may worship as they please. The Supreme Court has ruled that military service members retain their First Amendment rights, but that these rights can be limited due to military necessity: "the Court is not saying what military necessity is and under what conditions military commanders can evoke military necessity to limit the free exercise of religion. Currently, the interpretation and decision is determined by the commander."[60] The current policy on religious accommodation states that "requests for religious accommodation [. . .] will be approved when accommodation would not adversely affect mission accomplishment, including military readiness, unit cohesion, good order, discipline, health and safety, or any other military requirement."[61]

For Muslims in the military there are a few areas where the service member may seek religious accommodation: prayer, dietary restrictions, fasting, and grooming and attire.[62]

Prayer is something that comes up in several of the stories I will share in the coming chapters. When a Muslim refers to prayer, what is usually meant is *salah. Salah* is most commonly understood to be required five times a day and is formal and formulaic, involving ritual ablutions followed by the prayer ritual, which involves precise movements of the body combined with recitation of certain passages from the Qur'an and phrases in Arabic. A prayer mat is often used when praying. Each prayer is relatively quick (it can be completed in about five minutes), but the timing may prove complicated for those with strict work schedules. The first prayer is before dawn, the second around noon, then the late afternoon, sundown, and about ninety minutes after sundown.

In addition to daily prayers, many Muslims strive to attend communal prayers on Friday; this practice is referred to as *jummah*. The Friday service usually occurs around midday and involves gathering with other Muslims, listening to a short sermon (called a *khutbah*), and then praying. The entire service typically lasts an hour or less.

Islamic dietary guidelines are commonly understood to prohibit eating and drinking certain substances (most notably pork and alcohol) and consuming only meat that has been slaughtered in a specific way. This set of dietary restrictions is often referred to as halal. As with any religion, there is variation in how these guidelines are interpreted and practiced. Some Muslims may be very strict in their interpretation, eschewing even the use of alcohol in flavoring extracts and the like, while others may simply try to refrain from eating pork and/or drinking alcohol, and others do not follow these guidelines at all. Some of this variation appears in the stories I relate in the coming chapters. A service member unable to eat the food regularly served on base due to religious restrictions may be able to receive "com rats," extra cash to allow them to buy their own food. When in the field or at sea, halal (as well as kosher and vegetarian) MREs are available. These special MREs must be requested in advance; making sure that the unit deploys with the appropriate MREs is a part of the chaplain's responsibility.[63]

During the month of Ramadan, many Muslims fast. In Islamic practice, fasting involves abstaining from food, drink, and sexual relations from dawn until sunset. For service members, maintaining the Ramadan fast can be challenging. In the following chapters I will describe some of the various ways Muslim service members handle fasting.

Another area where religious accommodation issues may arise is grooming and attire standards. These were much less common concerns among the people who spoke with me.

Growing a beard is a common practice among civilian Muslims, but one that was, until quite recently, prohibited in the military, where men are required to be clean shaven. Muslim men may seek to wear a beard as a sunnah practice, meaning as a religious practice based on emulation of the Prophet Muhammad. Since the 1980s, service members seeking religious exceptions to regulations against beards have been denied. In 2009 a Sikh officer, Major Kamaljeet Singh Kalsi, was granted the first exception.[64] Since then, a few other Sikhs and Jews have also been granted permission; the expectation is that this will also open the way for Muslim service members to seek this accommodation.

Headwear is one of the most recognized signifiers of Islam in the United States. Some Muslim women cover their head with a *hijab*, or the head and face with a *niqab*. Muslim men may wear a skullcap called a *kufi* or *taqiyah*. Since 1988, following a contentious legal battle over the allowability of the Jewish yarmulke, service members have had the right to wear "neat and conservative" religious apparel while in uniform at the discretion of the service secretaries. As Hakim described (chapter 6), this has enabled Muslim men to wear their headgear. In 2014 this policy was revised to simplify the process of seeking accommodation for religious apparel.[65] While the skullcap worn by men has generally been accepted, religious head coverings for women have routinely been denied. The 2014 revision may make it more likely that women seeking to wear a *hijab* in uniform will be able to obtain permission to do so. The revised policy indicates that decisions will be made on a case-by-case basis.[66] The two women I spoke with did not seek to wear a *hijab* while in uniform. One of these women, Rahma (chapter 6), did wear a *hijab* when she was off duty and wears it now that she has left the military. She explains, "Outside of uniform I'll wear it, and I have always worn it. [. . .] You have your work time and you also have your downtime and I'd wear a scarf. Nobody had an issue with it, and if they did they didn't hang out with me and that was fine." We spoke a bit about how she came to this compromise of wearing a *hijab* out of uniform but not in uniform. She describes her reasoning:

> I have had some inner struggle with whether to wear the *hijab* or whether not to, but when I came to the choice to not wear it this was because I figured that the *hijab* [. . .] is all about modesty; modesty in behavior, modesty in dress. If you even look at the uniform, there ain't no cleavage there. Unless you get your uniform extra super-tight you're not going to see your booty either. I mean that's already modest itself. Modesty in behavior is a lot more important than modesty in dress, so that's what I chose to concentrate on. I chose to make

sure that I wasn't flirting with guys, I made sure I was always professional with them, and made sure I behave myself modestly and I'd watch out for that rather than worry about if I'm putting a piece of cloth on my head.

VIEWS OF ISLAM IN THE MILITARY

The context of the "War on Terror" shapes the relevance of Islam to the U.S. military. The U.S. military has been in Afghanistan since 2001. Afghanistan is predominantly Muslim and is well known for being controlled from 1996 to 2001 by the Taliban, a radically fundamentalist Islamist group. The U.S. military entered Afghanistan in pursuit of al-Qaeda, an Islamist terrorist organization. In 2003 the U.S. military invaded Iraq, a country with a population that is 97 percent Muslim, in pursuit of weapons of mass destruction. Since 2014 a new group that goes by the name "Islamic State" has committed acts of violence in the Middle East and has claimed responsibility for terrorist attacks in Europe and the United States. Given these conditions, it is inevitable that Islam has become a topic of interest in the military. The emphasis in these conflicts on "winning hearts and minds" has also highlighted issues of religious accommodation, for example the increased use of women soldiers to facilitate searching and communicating with Afghan and Iraqi women. For these reasons, Islam is a part of military education and training, and how it is depicted is likely to shape the experiences of Muslim service members. The general American population knows little about Islam, and so many people, whether civilians or service members, will adopt the perspective on Islam presented to them by "experts." The attitudes and approaches of these educators vary, and some clearly have very negative perspectives on Islam. It can be expected that Muslim service members in a unit where the education embraces negative stereotypes of Islam and Muslims will have a very different experience from those serving in a unit where education takes a neutral or positive view of Islam and Muslims.

As with many forms of education, what is taught depends on the particular instructor. Systematically assessing the attitudes and content of military education as it relates to Islam is beyond the scope of this project; however, media reports do indicate that at least some instructors hold negative stereotypes about Islam and Muslims.

In the previous chapter, I described two broad approaches to Islam: one neutral or positive and the other negative. Without a systematic investigation, there is no way to know how common these beliefs and attitudes are in the military. However, there is ample evidence that negative attitudes are at a minimum present in military intelligence and analysis. In the following section, I will briefly present some examples of negative stereotypes about Muslims being used by military educators or scholars. Daniel Pipes, who I introduced in the previous chapter, has taught at the U.S. Naval War College. He has clearly influenced other military analysts. For example, Mark Silinsky, who identifies himself as a "28-year veteran of the defense intelligence community," follows very clearly in Pipes's footsteps. Silinksy is quite open about his fear and loathing of Islam, writing "I make no apologies or qualifications for my article's thesis that Islam presents a danger to the US Armed Forces like none other."[67] He also argues that Islam should not be understood as a religion on a par with Christianity or Judaism, and he frequently publishes such inaccurate and inflammatory statements as:

> Much of Islam is predicated on violence, celebrates violence, and demands violence against non-Muslims. Verses in the holy Islamic text drip with the blood of beheadings, amputations, eye gouging, and mutilation.[68]

In April 2012 the Pentagon suspended a course, "Perspectives on Islam and Islamic Radicalism," at the Joint Forces Staff College in Norfolk, Virginia, after material used by the instructor, Lieutenant Colonel Matthew Dooley, became public. The course has been offered since 2004, and about 800 students have taken it.[69] The presentation in question used an explicit us-versus-them framework. "Your oath as a professional soldier forces you to pick a side here," reads text following a diagram that visually poses the U.S. Constitution and sharia in opposition.[70] Dooley taught that "Islam has already declared war on the West,"[71] and he advocated "Total War" as an appropriate response. In a proposed message from the U.S. Strategic Command (STRATCOM) he writes:

> [. . .] It is clear that Islam remains an ideology and system of governance that demands the extermination of anyone who does not subscribe to each and every one of its tenants [sic]. [. . .] Whether the United States chooses to declare war or not is no longer a relevant question. The fact that the US, and the western world in general, are in a fight for our very survival is a matter now intuitively obvious to any who have observed the basic, undisputed elements of Islam. [. . .] It is therefore time for the United States to make our true intentions clear. This barbaric ideology will no longer be tolerated. Islam must change

or we will facilitate its self-destruction. Let it be known that the United States remains, and will forever be, a beacon of freedom, self-determination, hope, and representative democracy. The American people will not be converted. We will not submit. We will not be intimidated, and we will not be driven from this earth.[72]

This curriculum clearly draws on the tradition of writers such as Pipes. It also uses historically familiar stereotypes. Dooley also neatly erases the millions of Muslim Americans in his framing.

Another example comes from a white paper published by the Air Force Research Laboratory in 2015. This report included a chapter by Tawfik Hamid, a self-described "Islamic thinker,"[73] in which the *hijab* is connected with terrorism. The *hijab* is described as "a catalyst for Islamism" that "contribute[s] to the idea of passive terrorism, which occurs when moderate segments of the population decline to speak against or actively resist terrorism."[74] In his model of the "Islamic Terrorism Cycle," the *hijab* is the only specific practice that he associates with the otherwise nebulous "Salafi" and "Islamist" terrorists, and he sees reducing the number of women who wear the *hijab* as a legitimate antiterrorism strategy, arguing anecdotally, "I have observed that, over the last few decades, terrorism was preceded by an increase in the prevalence of the hijab. In Sunni Muslim areas such as Kurdistan in Iraq, most women did not wear the hijab; these areas experienced fewer acts of terrorism than areas where the hijab was common, such as Al-Anbar Province."[75] He does not explain by what mechanism the *hijab* causes terrorism, though he does seem to argue that sexual deprivation causes suicide bombings, so perhaps his reasoning is related to this odd argument.

I am not claiming that all members of the military embrace this type of extreme ideology. There are likely many military educators who take a neutral or positive approach to Islam and refrain from making outrageous claims and statements and who consequently don't receive much public attention. What the preceding examples show is that familiar stereotypes promoting fear and hatred of Islam and Muslims can be found in the military, as in civilian society. Whether or not a particular service member or his or her colleagues or leaders have been exposed to these perspectives will likely shape the experiences of that service member.

In addition to the relevance of Islam to contemporary military missions, the role of Muslims in the U.S. military has been made prominent by the acts of violence committed by a few Muslim service members. There are three cases that have been well publicized and have prompted heated debate about the military service of Muslims. Chronologically, the first occurred on March 23, 2003, when Army Sergeant Hasan Akbar threw grenades into the tents of sleeping soldiers in Kuwait, killing two officers. The second, and most widely reported, incident occurred on November 5, 2009, when Army psychiatrist Major Nidal Malik Hassan opened fire at Fort Hood, killing thirteen people. Most recently, on July 27, 2011, Army Private Naser Abdo was arrested outside Fort Hood. At the time of his arrest he was staying in a motel room that contained a handgun, directions for building a bomb from an al-Qaeda publication, and the supplies to build a bomb.

In addition to these cases where the service member was undoubtedly guilty of committing (or intending to commit) violence, there have been other cases where accusations were made against Muslim service members that were later dismissed. For example, Army Chaplain James Yee, a Muslim chaplain working at Guantanamo Bay, was arrested on September 10, 2003, and charged with sedition and espionage. Yee was held for seventy-six days before all charges were dropped. He subsequently received an Article 15[76] for adultery and storage of pornography on a government computer. He denies all the charges.[77]

Hakim, who I will introduce fully in chapter 6, brought up the case of Chaplain Yee in our discussion:

> It does bother me when I see [Yee's] case being utilized as an example. That is an injustice to do that without giving the full story and conclusion that he was found not guilty of any of [the charges]. So we've had these incidences in the military by certain individuals but when you contrast [. . .] that with tens of thousands of Muslims who have served honorably and with distinction, you know we have Muslim soldiers who [. . .] have died in the line of duty. Some of them are buried at Arlington cemetery. And so their legacy and what they've done cannot be dismissed because of a few who have done just the opposite.

Building on this fear of Muslims in the military, the King hearings, which I described in the previous chapter, also focused on the special "problem" of Muslims in the military and included a joint hearing of the House Committee on Homeland Security and the Senate Homeland Security and Governmental Affairs Committee dedicated to "The Threat to Military Communities Inside the United States." Within this hearing, one of the areas of emphasis was on the "insider threat," that is, the threat supposedly posed by Muslims in the military.

IMPORTANCE OF DIVERSITY

Diversity has several benefits for the U.S. military. Diversity is crucial for the social legitimacy of the U.S. military. Because the military is a powerful social institution that controls the legitimate uses of violence, civilian society prefers a military that resembles the society as a whole. In the United States, this means a diverse force. While the military led civilian society in racial integration, it has lagged behind civilian society with respect to gender and sexuality integration, and the heated debates about this topic demonstrate the importance of diversity in maintaining social legitimacy.

In purely practical terms, the successful integration of diverse personnel can improve performance. Throughout history, the U.S. military has recruited minority populations to meet personnel needs, so the ability to integrate these new populations into the military is crucial for military effectiveness. In addition to helping meet personnel needs, diversity is also a powerful asset in the globalized marketplace. Diversity brings new perspectives and approaches.

The Department of Defense has come to embrace the importance of diversity as evidenced by the 2012–2017 Department of Defense's Diversity and Inclusion Strategic Plan, which included the following:

> We defend the greatest nation in the world—a democracy founded on the promise of opportunity for all. It is a nation whose demographic makeup parallels the environment in which we live—continually changing—and DoD must change to maintain and sustain its future forces. To the degree we truly represent our democracy, we are a stronger and more relevant force. The Department views diversity as a strategic imperative. Diverse backgrounds and experiences bring inherently different outlooks and ways of thinking, the key to innovation in organizations. We gain a strategic advantage by leveraging the diversity of all members and creating an inclusive environment in which each member is valued and encouraged to provide ideas critical to innovation, optimization, and organizational mission success.[78]

As an institution deeply involved in international operations, the U.S. military can also benefit from the reservoirs of cultural competence that are maintained in a diverse force. Cultural competence is the ability to work effectively with individuals and groups from other cultures, and the importance of this skill set is increasingly being realized in contemporary military missions. Cultural competence may refer to in-depth experience with a specific culture or a broader adaptability that allows one to move between multiple cultures. The operations in Afghanistan and Iraq have required U.S. troops to work in close proximity with non-Western military and civilian populations. The nature of these operations and the emphasis on "winning hearts and minds" requires a nuanced understanding of cultural differences.

Figuring out how to address cultural competence has been an ongoing challenge for the military. In a thesis written for the U.S. Army Command and General Staff College, Edward Healey Jr. notes that military cultural training commonly includes a checklist of dos and don'ts, some phrases of Arabic, and a simplified historical overview. This level of preparation is unlikely to be of much use: "This level of cultural awareness training may be enough to keep a Marine or soldier out of jail in a foreign land, but it does little to increase the likelihood of accomplishing the military mission."[79] For example, in February 2012, American troops burned surplus Qur'ans at Bagram Air Base in Afghanistan, triggering violent riots and attacks on U.S. troops. These soldiers had been provided with a list of "don'ts" for handling the Qur'an but nothing was mentioned about burning it. This example demonstrates the weakness of training that tries to distill culture into a list of rules. Montgomery McFate, an anthropologist who has worked with the U.S. Department of Defense, explained, "It makes culture into a set of arbitrary rules. You don't understand why [. . .]. The Bible is not considered itself a holy object, and unless you'd grown up in a religious tradition where that was true, you wouldn't understand the way that Muslims feel about the Koran."[80]

Language and culture skills are not inherently tied to ethnic or religious identity. Non-Muslims are capable of learning languages and cultures associated with Islam, just as some Muslims have no linguistic or cultural fluency in these areas. However, within the current educational and social culture of the United States, many of these skills are concentrated within the Muslim community. In 2009, 35,083 students studied Arabic at 466 institutions of higher education in the United States. Of these enrollments only 13.6 percent were advanced enrollments. To put this in perspective, Arabic enrollments account for only 2 percent of all foreign language enrollments. Spanish, the language with the highest enrollment, had 864,986 students; Chinese had 60,976. Other languages relevant to the current military missions are even less accessible to students in the United States. In 2009, 974 students studied Urdu, while only 114 students studied Pashto.[81] Interest in these regions and languages is increasing, but implementing academic programs takes time, and achieving linguistic and cultural fluency requires years of study. As these programs develop, many of the needed language and culture skills must be sought among those who learned them from their family and community: that is, Muslim Americans.

SUMMARY

The U.S. military has a long history of integrating new groups of people into the ranks. Decisions to increase the participation of minority groups are often driven by the practical need for personnel, but they can also be shaped by social conditions in the civilian world. There are certain characteristics of the U.S. military that can facilitate this integration. For example, the emphasis on hierarchy provides a way to enforce inclusive behavior. The military can even use its structure to provide a level of protection for minority service members, for example, by eliminating or mitigating racial differences in pay that are found in the civilian world.

While many of these positive effects can be seen in the history of blacks in the U.S. military, for other social groups, pressure from civilian society was needed for their inclusion in the military. For example, for LGBT service members, a changing tide in public opinion pushed President Barack Obama and the military to revisit exclusionary policies. For women, we see a combination of these approaches. Women's service has been shaped both by the changing needs of the military and by changes in civilian society. In particular, the decision to open combat roles to women came at the intersection of these factors. Women have been proving valuable additions to units in combat conditions in Afghanistan and Iraq; at the same time, public opinion has shifted toward the greater inclusion of women.

The practical role of diversity in the military is also worth noting. In addition to needing personnel, the military needs specific skills. In the contemporary conflicts, as well as the likely conflicts to come, soft skills, such as cultural competence, are necessary for mission success. Maintaining a diverse force increases the likelihood that the military will have access to particular language and culture skills that are becoming so important.

THREE

INTRODUCING THE RANGE
OF EXPERIENCES

Muslims in the military have many different experiences. Although there are
some common factors that seem to shape these experiences, differences in personality, background, and the particulars of the unit they serve in create a range
of experiences, demonstrating that being Muslim in the military can mean very
different things. In this chapter I'll introduce four people who highlight how
diverse the experiences of Muslims in the military can be. Mahmood and Kareem
had generally positive experiences during their military service, while Sadia
and Farid are on the opposite end with some of the most negative experiences
described by the people who spoke with me.

MAHMOOD: MEET A MUSLIM IN THE MILITARY

I met with Mahmood in the lobby of the apartment building where he had recently moved with his wife after one of the relocations that military families are
so familiar with. When I spoke with him, Mahmood had been in the military
for ten years and planned to stay another decade, at which point he will be enti-
tled to retired pay.[1] Recently married and in the middle of his career, Mahmood
was successfully balancing the demands of the military with the expectations
of family and community. I introduce Mahmood first because his reasons for
joining the military, his experiences while serving, and his general satisfaction
were common among the people who spoke with me.

Mahmood immigrated to the United States from South Asia as a teenager
and followed in the footsteps of his father and brother, who both served in the

military. His decision to join the military was influenced by family, opportunities for travel, and the military lifestyle. When I asked him what made him decide to join the military, he responded:

> Because of my brother, and [. . .] I wanted to see the world and it seemed like the military [would give me that], and the camaraderie of the guys and all this kind of stuff.

He went on to explain how being an immigrant to the United States also shaped his decision:

> This is my new home, and I think joining the military is the right thing to do, whatever country you're in. I feel that's how you can serve your country and the United States has been awesome, excellent to myself and my family. I feel like the country's given me so much and I am doing my share to pay back sort of.

Mahmood's answer reflects some of the common reasons many people join the armed forces: family tradition, the opportunity for self-improvement, and patriotism and a sense of service.

Mahmood's answer—and ultimately the answers I got from all of the people who spoke with me—was not quite what I expected based on the history I had studied in preparation for these interviews. Unlike what I had read about the experiences of Japanese Americans serving (or being excluded from serving) in World War II, Mahmood did not talk about his military service as a way for him to prove that he is a loyal American. Despite the tense post-9/11 atmosphere, Muslims were never explicitly told they could not serve. For Mahmood, unlike for many Japanese Americans, military service was not something he had to fight for; it was always an option open to him, and he chose this option for the same reasons most Americans choose it.

Mahmood was aware of the complex environment he was in as a Muslim serving in the U.S. military in a post-9/11 world. He knew that being Muslim could be used against him, and he did recognize that his service to the country is a defense against this. When I asked him if he was proud to be in the military, he responded:

> Yeah, I really am actually. Especially with the kind of political stuff going on, I don't feel like anybody can say anything to me. [. . .] I don't think anybody can question my patriotism or something like that.

Although Mahmood recognizes that being Muslim in post-9/11 America can at times be complex, he does not feel that being Muslim had any impact on his decade of service.

> I don't think it's like anything different than being non-Muslim. [. . .] I mean, with all these conflicts going on maybe you could have a thing like stuff's going on in every Muslim country, [. . .] [but] that's more political. Personally, being a Muslim in the military hasn't really, I don't think, affected me.

This became a theme as I spoke with Muslim service members and veterans. Many recognized that being Muslim mattered in some ways, but felt it did not impact their military careers.

For example, Mahmood related a story of how being Muslim came up in his everyday life in the military, but how he did not see this as indicating anything negative about being Muslim in the military:

> The military is not PC [politically correct] at all, so I get teased about doing things [. . .] you know some of my friends call me a terrorist or I'm going to blow myself up. It's completely different, it's not some redneck making some joke at me. So there'll be that kind of teasing back and forth and all this kind of stuff going on [. . .] But I don't want you to get [the idea] that I was picked upon because I'm Muslim because that wasn't the case at all. [. . .] That teasing goes on with everyone basically. You've gotta have a thick skin in the military, and it wasn't personal, I don't want you to think that.

Mahmood recognized that relating a story of being called a "terrorist" by his colleagues may seem like a negative experience, but he was quick to explain to me that this was not the case. Building on his repeated assertion that he didn't want me to get the wrong idea, let me place this story within the broader context of military culture. As he explained, and as has been documented,[2] in military culture, this type of ribbing is normal. When kept within the realm of friendly joshing, this simply indicates solid camaraderie. That Mahmood's colleagues included him by teasing him about being Muslim is paradoxically a sign that they saw him as part of the team. In this case, not being teased would be a way of excluding him. Being teased is a sign of inclusion, and because cohesion is strong and the teasers are known and trusted, the interaction is friendly rather than malicious.

Until recently Mahmood did not consider himself to be a devout Muslim. Recently he has been striving to become more observant:

I don't wanna come off as being a super-religious, pious person because I have not been. [But] now I'm trying to be, like praying and stuff like that.

At the time we spoke, Mahmood had never sought formal religious accommodation, and he was generally uncertain if his experiences would have been the same if he had been more observant. As we spoke, he explored the hypothetical, but ultimately concluded that religious observance would not have changed his experience much:

Now if I were super-religious and strict I don't know what my experiences would've been like in the unit, if it would've caused friction or whatever the case may be. But being the way I was, people knew I was Muslim but I kinda did the stuff that I'm not supposed to—like drinking and all that, so it didn't really make that much of a difference because of how I acted. Now if I was completely following every rule that I'm supposed to, I don't know if it would've been different or not. But I don't know if it would've been because, I mean, you can go pray in your car or something, so it's not like I'd be pitching the prayer mat in the middle of the room, so the only thing that I'd be doing differently is probably not drinking and there's plenty of people that are not Muslims who do not drink and it's not like they were excluded, so I don't think it would've made a difference even if I was a more practicing Muslim than I was.

Interestingly, while he argued that abstaining from alcohol would not be unique and so could be done without much comment, he saw prayer as something that is best practiced in the private sphere, hidden from his colleagues. Several of the people I spoke with talked about prayer in this way. Since the military is not a secular institution where discomfort would be expected from any religious expression, this suggests that certain expressions of faith are more accepted than others.

There are several possible reasons prayer was treated as something to be hidden while fasting was never talked about by my respondents this way. One is the familiarity of fasting to others within the Christian norms of American society. Fasting is a practice that is found in Christianity (and Judaism), and although what is meant by "fasting" differs (many Christian fasts allow drinking water, while Islamic fasting does not), the general practice is familiar. On the other hand, the ritual prayer of *salah* is seen as foreign to Christian tradition. It is very different from contemporary Christian prayer, which tends to be less frequent, more personalized, and requires only minor bodily movements (folding hands, crossing arms, kneeling, etc.).[3] Additionally, prayer, regardless of denomination, is often seen as a private matter in the United States.

Fasting and prayer are also very different in their popular associations. Ramadan may be recognizable due to media coverage as an "exotic" but celebratory event. Because Ramadan is celebrated in many Islamic countries with confections and decorations, the images in the media are comfortingly cheery. *Salah*, however, is often associated in the media with the idea of Islam as violent and "other." The former communications professor Jack Shaheen considered the portrayal of Arabs and Muslims in Hollywood movies and noted how images of Muslim prayer are often used in association with violent villains: "When mosques are displayed onscreen, the camera inevitably cuts to Arabs praying, and then gunning down civilians. Such scenarios are common fare."[4]

While prayer and social restrictions have not factored heavily into his military experiences, Mahmood did observe the month-long fast of Ramadan. Two strategies emerged from my interviews with regard to fasting. One approach, which Mahmood did not take, is to modify military duties to accommodate the fast. This strategy involves seeking formal accommodation, and includes things such as rescheduling physical training or altering working hours. Mahmood used the opposite strategy; he adapted his religious practice to the demand of the missions of the day.

> On the days when I had [certain duties] I didn't fast basically. So it's not like I was going to have the schedule changed for me, so I just decided not to fast on the days I had [these duties] [. . .]. If I could do it then I did, and if I didn't think I could do it I just didn't fast.

The military lifestyle has been a good fit for Mahmood, and he has enjoyed his service, adapting with humor to the annoyances it can present:

> Yeah I like [military life]. I've enjoyed the moving around, though it gets kind of old because your stuff's damaged. We just moved here, we're missing three couches [laughs].

Reflecting upon his ten years of service, he had only positive things to say:

> You know, I can't really think of a bad experience. I mean, [boot camp] was miserable, but now looking back it was fun. [The drill instructor would] yell

"Get in the dirt! Get in the grass!" Basically doing a lot of push-ups, just doing physical stuff and the whole time I'd kind of be thinking, "Wow, we're getting yelled at by this drill sergeant, it's kinda like a movie." And so it was stressful because there's no time and you've got to do a lot of stuff, but now looking back I only have good memories of it.

Overall Mahmood had positive experiences in the military. He found the military to be a good fit for his personality and felt that his religious identity had little effect on his experiences in the military.

SADIA: LIFE UNDER INVESTIGATION

I met Sadia by luck. I was at a lecture and got into a conversation with the person sitting next to me about this project. She got me in touch with Sadia, who happily invited me to her home to talk. Sadia is a practicing Muslim; however, as a white convert she is not automatically seen by others as Muslim due to her name or appearance. Sadia left the military after a five-year career, and her experiences were some of the most negative I heard. I introduce her here as a contrast to Mahmood and to illustrate the range of experiences.

Sadia joined the military on a whim after high school and intended to make it a career. She is a good example of what psychologists Elizabeth Ginexi, Alison Miller, and Steve Tarver refer to as a "flounderer." They identified various motivations for joining the military, but also identified "flounderers" which they describe this way: "the visit to the recruiter and subsequent decision to enlist was completely unplanned and extremely abrupt. These individuals' goals were very unclear [. . .] these individuals appeared to have been waiting for something to happen in their lives yet had lacked the initiative or motivation to alter their present situations."[5] Sadia's description of her decision to join the military fits this:

It was sorta random, and I woke up one day and decided to do it. It was the best and worst decision I ever made [laughs], but it worked out in the end.

As we started talking, Sadia told me that she generally fit in well with the military lifestyle. She had family members who had served and was familiar with the demands of military life, though she did not attribute her decision to join to her family history:

When I was little I wanted to join the military cause my mom was in the military before I was born and my dad was in the military. I mean a lot of people when they ask me why I joined the military I would cite that, "Oh it's just a family tradition," when really I just woke up that day was like you know, it's a Tuesday, I think I'm gonna join the military.

Her family was generally supportive of her decision to join the military; the main source of concern was her decision to enlist rather than seek a commission:

My mom actually, she was not thrilled. She told me to go officer, and I was like psssh, officer, I don't even know how you would go officer. I don't know, I never looked into it.

Sadia enjoyed the training and education she received in the military, and like many of the people who spoke with me, she enjoyed the way the military broadened her horizons, including introducing her to her current husband. Sadia saw becoming Muslim as the catalyst that led to her leaving the military: "Like it was pretty good until I became Muslim."

Sadia characterized her conversion to Islam as being similar to her decision to join the military: "It was all sort of accidental." Raised "Christian in the loose sense of the word," Sadia came to identify as a Catholic as an adult:

I just decided to be Catholic 'cause I really liked their churches; they're very pretty. And so if you're going to sit there and be bored for an hour it might as well be pretty inside, so that's how I picked Catholic.

At some point after she joined the military, she was given a Qur'an; she no longer remembers the details of how she came by this book or what prompted her to begin reading it. "I must have been stuck somewhere and really, really bored, 'cause it looked really like not something I wanted to read." She told me about how what she read sparked something for her:

So then, in the second chapter of the Qur'an it says the Christian, the Jews, anybody who believes in one God and does good deeds, they'll go to heaven. I'm like "Oh this is nice, I like this." So that's kinda what turned me.

She spent about a week regularly visiting with a Christian base chaplain to explore Christian and Islamic theology before deciding that "I like the Muslim answers, so I'm gonna go with it."

Despite her early positive experiences in the military, Sadia told me that her conversion and new Muslim identity were taken as evidence of her untrustworthiness. Sadia spent two years under investigation, during which time she was removed from her skilled position, lost her security clearance, and was given temporary secretarial work. She told me this all began when her ex-husband made a false report following a domestic dispute. At the time she converted to Islam, Sadia was married to a non-Muslim man who did not take well to her conversion. She described married life after her conversion: "He was very not ok with me becoming Muslim, and he was very angry." Their marital tension came to a head while out at a restaurant. Wanting to avoid a public fight at the table, Sadia went to her car and locked herself inside:

> Our food hadn't gotten there yet so I just, I'm not gonna fight in a public place and I'm not gonna sit there and take that, so I just got up and left and [went to] my car [. . .] He ran after me and tried to get in and that didn't work. He said "Unlock this door!" and I said "Nope."

The situation in the parking lot escalated:

> That's what he was really mad about, I wouldn't unlock the door. We were sitting in [the parking lot] and he's like, "If you keep acting this way I will beat you, I will *beat* you."

After this fight Sadia's husband went to stay with friends, and he was dismayed when Sadia ended the relationship:

> He was upset, he was very angry and then I gave him all his stuff back [. . .] and I gave him back his ring and so he was very angry, and he went in to the commander the next day and said I was a terrorist.

At the end of an all-night shift, Sadia was told to report to her commander. Thinking it was to receive praise for an extraordinary test score she had recently received, she was shocked when her commander accused her of disloyalty:

> I got in ridiculous amounts of trouble. Like "Oh, you know you've been doing this and you've been doing that so we're putting you under special investigation" and stuff like that and I'm like what!?! Like me seriously shaking. They escorted me off the base and that was pretty much the beginning of the end for me.

She told me she was confused and in a state of disbelief:

The investigation was horrible 'cause I didn't really grasp that they were serious. They were accusing me of funneling information and stuff to the enemy and clearly I'm not doing that. I know that, and they know that I wasn't doing it.

During the course of the investigation Sadia was under surveillance, and she noticed strange cars following her. "And then later I'd see the pictures of myself doing random things." Her security clearance was suspended, and she was re-assigned to administrative work. This reassignment added to her stress:

I was exceptional at my [previous] job, and then they sent me out to do these other things, and I had no idea what they were doing 'cause everything has to be micromanaged and you have to fill out all these special forms and you have to do all these different rules and stuff and they have nothing to do with anything I'd been trained to do. It was very irritating for me.

After she was removed from her job, rumors began flourishing:

It was hilarious. [My colleagues said] I got sent to Guantanamo, I was in Leavenworth, I went crazy and was in an institution. [. . .] 'cause I wasn't allowed back [in the office], I just disappeared one day and so you know the rumor mill. I was still in the dorms though! Those people lived there, like how did they not see me?

This atmosphere of gossip and rumor is particularly telling. Without knowing any of the details of the accusations against Sadia from the military's point of view, a unit that so easily devolves into rumor and gossip may say something about the quality of the cohesion in this unit and the willingness of leadership to tolerate this toxic environment. It is also clear that however this atmosphere came about, this unit was neither supportive of its absent colleague nor anticipating her return. That she no longer belonged seems to have been accepted long before the investigation was concluded.

The stress of being under suspicion also had negative health effects on Sadia, which she described:

I was having panic attacks; I'd forget where I was; I'd forget where I lived. I would completely black out, you could ask me what planet I was on and I'd not be able to tell you.

Despite having planned to make the military a career, this experience convinced Sadia to leave the military and left her with negative feelings about the military:

> I signed for six [years] originally 'cause I assumed that I'd stay in forever, that I'd stay in until they kicked me out 'cause I was too old and crusty. And yeah, so I love them a little less now.

Since leaving the military, Sadia has become an anti-spokesperson for military service. "I wouldn't recommend it for somebody else. I would not. And people I meet they say they're gonna join whatever branch, I say don't do it."

Specific leadership seemed to play a central role in Sadia's story. Sadia noted that other religious minorities, such as Latter-Day Saints, were also singled out for negative treatment:

> I mean it's not exclusive to Muslims, like I worked with a Mormon girl, [. . .] she took a lot of abuse. [. . .] They hated her because she was Mormon and you know they were otherwise generic Christian or probably not practicing or anything, but since you're not their flavor they are angry about it. And so before I came she was public enemy number one.

Troubling tendencies like these in the atmosphere of her unit suggest that weak leadership may have been an issue.

While many of the people who spoke with me talked about intentionally praying in private, Sadia used her in-limbo status to make her prayers public.

> I'm like whatever. I'm already under investigation; they're claiming they think I'm a terrorist, what else are they going to do? So I'd pray at work, just get my little rug out and bam right there in the middle, which upset a lot of people. At the last place I got farmed out to, there was one guy I could tell it really bugged him. I was like whatever, I don't care about you.

Sadia's experiences illustrate the negative side of military service that some Muslims experience. While those people I spoke with who had positive experiences felt that their identity as a Muslim did not affect their career, for Sadia, her identity did have an effect. The way she described her leadership also illuminates an important factor in understanding why there is so much difference in experience. A strong leader can maintain a healthy and diverse unit, while a weak or destructive leader can tear a unit apart.

KAREEM: MILITARY CULTURE SHIFTS

When we spoke, Kareem was no longer in the military. Kareem was a teenager when he and his family immigrated to the United States from the Arab world. After completing high school, he joined the military as a machinist. As with many of the people who spoke with me, Kareem felt that the opportunities available in the military were excellent. It was these opportunities that led him to join and enticed him to remain for more than a decade.

> Initially I just wanted to travel and experience new things away from home, the travel, money for college basically. The plan was to do it for four years and get out but I decided I liked it too much; I stayed in for eleven years.

For Kareem's father, military service was not a part of the life he envisioned for his son in the United States.

> My dad's main concern was how is this going to fit in with your school 'cause my father came to the U.S. to study and do his grad school here in the U.S., so he values education very much, so his main concern was no, you go to school, you finish your undergrad, you go to grad school, then you get a good job, then you buy a house, then you get married and that's the track of life he had imagined for me.

The story of Kareem's family's immigration is quite common among American Muslims. With the revision of immigration laws in 1965, immigration from the Islamic world increased and became characterized by high levels of education and ambition; it "included a large number of highly educated, socially mobile, professional Muslims—part of the Arab and South Asian 'brain drain.'"[6] For Kareem's parents, and for many immigrant Muslim parents, a specific trajectory is expected for their children that emphasizes education and family. Serving in the military, and particularly choosing to serve in the military before or instead of attending college, is a serious deviation from the expectations of many parents within this community.[7] Kareem also thought that military service might also be viewed unfavorably because it could encourage a lifestyle at odds with religious and cultural expectations.

> I'm sure the reason why [my father] was against me joining the military was he thought a nineteen-year-old boy wanted to leave home and his immediate thought was "Oh this guy wants to party."

Despite the reservations of his family, Kareem joined the military. Kareem found the military to be highly rewarding and full of opportunities.

The military was extremely good to me; I would say that the military was my rich daddy. There was no question, whatever I wanted to do I could totally do it. I'd say, "Military, daddy, I wanna travel" and [the military] sent me everywhere, or allowed me to go everywhere, provided me with the opportunity to go everywhere [. . .] I said, "Oh, I want to go to school for this"; they'd send me to school for that. [. . .] It was an incredible opportunity. I have absolutely nothing bad to say about the military. No regrets whatsoever even though I joined at a young age. I could've wasted my life on booze and party but I didn't. I think the military is what you make out of it.

Kareem took advantage of all the opportunities he could during his time in the military, but after eleven years he was ready to pursue opportunities in the civilian world and he left the military.

Kareem identified himself as a moderately practicing Muslim:

I wasn't a very good Muslim on active duty. I didn't pray five times a day, that's really the only thing that I didn't really observe. I didn't really drink . . . I didn't really drink, I'll keep it there [laughs]. I didn't really drink, I didn't eat pork, I fasted Ramadan.

As with Mahmood, Kareem did not seek out accommodation for the Ramadan fast. However, as a teenager at the beginning of his career, he took pride in completing the fast under physically strenuous conditions.

Working in [a] 120, 130 degree room and fasting that was very challenging, so after breaking the fast I'd have to drink a lot of water. I was 19, 20 years old so my body took it very well back then; I was a strong young man. But today I don't think I'd be able to fast in that environment.

Kareem's approach of not modifying either his military or religious duties was not a common one among the people who spoke with me, though another person spoke with great admiration about a story on his base of a young man who had allegedly done the same. I assumed this story was an urban legend until Kareem shared his experience, showing that it was possible.

Kareem did not feel that being Muslim had any negative effects on his military career.

There weren't really any, like I can't remember too many challenges for me as a Muslim in the military except maybe the few times I'll go up to the chow hall and find out that the main course today is either pork chops or ham [laughs]. And I'm like what the F, I guess no meat for me today. I'll eat the rice or the noodles or some kind of gravy. I always find a way to adapt and overcome.

Kareem connected this occasional issue with food to a military culture in the 1990s that was less cognizant of these everyday aspects of diversity than it is today.

When I'd bring that up to the leadership, they'd be like "What!? You eat whatever is available, son," because people just were not aware. But then eventually people became more sensitive I think to the different kinds of people within the military, it's not just white or black anymore, you have a lot of different people in the military.

Kareem began his service before 9/11, and he talked about seeing a shift in both military and civilian perceptions of Islam and Muslims:

The awareness of the simple American [shifted], not just the simple [service member], of what a Muslim is, or may be. I'll call it the paranoia factor, the Muslim paranoia. Yeah that really started up in 2001. [. . .] I think today people are more aware, they know brown people are dangerous, people from the Middle East are dangerous, people who are different, Middle East, Far East yeah that's all the same. Muslim, Sikh, Baha'i, Hindu, they really don't know the difference. The average American still does not know the difference. All they know is that Middle East, Far East, oh terrorist. They really don't know.

Kareem noted that while people were more aware of "brown" people, a great deal of ignorance remained.

People really honestly did not know what the hell Arab is. [. . .] Occasionally I'd say I'm Arab and people would say, "Oh my God, my next door neighbor's from Bangladesh, you should totally get together." [. . .] They actually thought that people from Bangladesh, people from Afghanistan, people from Libya and Morocco [are the same]; they all speak the same language, they all eat kebabs, cool.

For Kareem, it was obvious that attitudes in the civilian world would permeate the military.

The military, it's a small society in itself so the factors of society are very well represented in the military as a whole, so there are racist people in the military.

However, the military provided unique protections through hierarchy and an emphasis on equality of opportunity:

So there are racist people in the military but they have to abide by the rules because we have equal opportunity committees and all that, all those programs that make sure that everybody's treated fairly. So there are racist people but they have to play by the rules.

Kareem also noted that the military culture was designed to emphasize cohesion and a sense of belonging among service members. This created a sense of community that was larger than racial, ethnic, or religious differences.

We are taught one thing from very early on is that there's only one color and that's [the color of the uniform]. [. . .] So yeah, there are no whites or blacks or browns or Hispanics or whatever, we're all service members, we're all on the same team, and that's one thing we were taught from very early on.

Kareem had generally positive experiences in the military, though he did observe some increased tensions after 9/11. We also talked a bit about some tensions in civilian Muslim communities. Within some Muslim communities there is resistance to the idea of serving in the U.S. military, and particularly being involved in the conflicts in Iraq and Afghanistan. For example, one of Sirin and Fine's respondents exclaimed during a focus group, "We're all mad at [my cousin]. He joined the Army! the U.S. Army to fight in Iraq!!!"[8] The Pew Research Center also reports lower levels of support for the U.S. invasion of Afghanistan among the American Muslim population. In 2011 only 38 percent of Muslims felt that the use of force in Afghanistan was the right decision, compared with 57 percent of the general population.[9]

There are various reasons for this resistance; Kareem's family was opposed to his service because it did not meet their expectations of what he should do and because they were concerned it would lead him to make poor life choices. Another source of resistance that may keep Muslims from joining the military are perceptions of what the military does. Of particular concern is the idea that service in the military will entail killing other Muslims. Kareem had encountered some of these opinions, and we spent some time discussing differences in opinion within the Muslim community:

People interpret Islam differently. Some are more fundamentalist than others. Some will say the Sheik bin Laden,[10] others will say the terrorist bin Laden. So the ones that say Sheik bin Laden are the ones that'll say the military is *haraam* [forbidden/sinful].[11] "We will not participate in any campaign that kills Muslims, that's *haraam*." I participate in campaigns that kill bad Muslims, you know. If it walks like a duck, if it quacks like a duck, it's a duck. A terrorist organization is a terrorist organization [. . .] It's like no, we don't just go and kill Muslims, we kill bad Muslims, period. We don't just go and bomb Sheik Muhammad the peaceful guy who leads people at prayers on Friday, no. We will however conduct a campaign and get the guy who killed thousands and thousands of people and drop him in the ocean, yeah. We're not bad guys for doing that.

Kareem thought the use of monolithic categories based on religious identity to be intellectually lazy when used by Muslims or non-Muslims. Just as he disparaged those who think all Muslims are the same, he also expressed disdain for Muslims who do not recognize radical and violent elements within their global communities.

The ones I have a problem with are those who have a problem with the military, particularly because they kill Muslims, and to me these people are no different from the average redneck, forgive my [language], who doesn't know the difference, this is an Arab, this is a Pakistanian [intentional mispronunciation], they're all the same, they're all raghead. The Muslims who don't make the distinction between good Muslims and bad Muslims, or violent fundamentalist Muslims and good Muslims, are no different from those ignorant rednecks who have no idea. To them Muslims are Muslims, bad or good they're all brothers and sisters. I beg to differ.

Overall Kareem had positive experiences in the military. He felt that the military offered him many opportunities, and he found his experiences rewarding. Kareem noted the diversity of backgrounds of those serving and saw EO policies and a clear system to address problems that could arise from such diversity as an important characteristic of the military. These policies provided a level of security; everyone has to "play by the rules." This structure allows service members to construct a shared identity based on their commonality as members of a specific service branch. Kareem also commented on a changing atmosphere around diversity issues in the military. While he did note increased tensions around being Muslim in both the civilian and military communities following 9/11, he also noticed increased awareness and accommodation.

FARID: FAMILY TARGETED

The story Farid shared with me illustrates the extreme negative end of the range of experiences. Farid shared a deeply personal and tragic story that illustrates the costs Muslim service members may bear for their service. This account is part of a larger narrative; however, for confidentiality reasons I am separating this story from the rest of the narrative and will refer here to this respondent as Farid. Farid is a South Asian immigrant with family still living abroad. In the United States, Farid is well known in his community, having regularly appeared on local television shows to denounce terrorism and al-Qaeda in particular. It is this prominence, he believes, that led to his being threatened by a stranger while at a Muslim store:

> [Before I deployed to Afghanistan] I took [my mother] to the [halal] butcher. [As we were standing in line] the guy next to me turned to me and he said, "What's the difference between a chicken and a traitor?" He said it with a big smile, so I thought it was some sort of a joke, [laughs]. "I don't know, tell me the difference between a chicken and a traitor." And he said "The chickens first we kill and then we skin, but the traitors first we skin and then we kill." And then he walked away. And suddenly I was frozen [. . .] for like one millisecond I couldn't speak, I couldn't move. [. . .] I told my commander [. . .] but the next thing I know I'm on a plane to Afghanistan.

While he was deployed in Afghanistan, his uncle in Pakistan was murdered after publicly discussing the possibility of Farid coming to give a lecture.

> [. . .] Nobody ever told me that al-Qaeda did it, but just the coincidence. He was an old man, never harmed anyone, nothing was stolen from his home. So one of the theories was that he was pushing me, an American soldier, to go back and give a lecture on terrorism and al-Qaeda's position was we don't need a lecture on terrorism from this man's nephew, especially someone who is so against us.

More devastating, Farid's father was subsequently murdered in Pakistan:

[My father] wasn't shy about showing off that his son was an American soldier. And then one day I got the news that he was dead. When I looked into it I could not get any details; the best I can get is the local newspaper [. . .] The headline was that he had been tortured and killed and [. . .] nobody wants to talk about it. His own brother, I said, "Can you give me the death certificate?" And he said, "I'm not going anywhere near this case." And the only thing that can arouse such fear and intimidation is if al-Qaeda had done it. [. . .] Nothing was stolen from his home and he was tortured. In robberies nobody's tortured. [. . .] When I heard all that, it made me ill for a week [. . .] I have other relatives there. They killed my uncle then they killed my father and I just didn't know if they could kill somebody else.

While Muslim service members, particularly those with ties to communities abroad, can provide vital cultural competence to the U.S. military, this contribution can have dire consequences for the individual and his or her family. For al-Qaeda and similar groups, Americans (both civilians and service members) are identified as targets. The religion of a service member does not protect them; in fact, a Muslim choosing to serve in "Satan's US troops"[12] may be viewed even more negatively than a non-Muslim doing so. Such a decision may be seen as being a traitor, as in the threat made against Farid. This is an aspect of fighting terrorism that leadership in the military should be aware of and seek to address. It is a complex problem without an obvious solution: those service members who may be in the most danger due to their identity and cultural and familial ties are also the ones who are most needed for those same reasons.

FOUR

THE IMPORTANCE OF LEADERSHIP

As I spoke with people about their experiences and reflected on the stories people were sharing, it became clear that leadership was a crucial variable in understanding the experiences of Muslims in the military. Leadership involves using social influence to get a group of people to accomplish a given goal. Leadership is a central component of U.S. military culture, and it plays a crucial role in the success or failure of efforts to integrate diversity in the force. The sociologists Mady Segal and Chris Bourg argue that "the degree to which the organization accomplishes successful integration of previously excluded groups is a function of leadership commitment to that integration at all levels."[1] Leaders shape both the behavior and atmosphere of the unit as it relates to diversity, tolerance, and integration. Leaders serve as role models, shaping the behavior of other members. They also directly shape behavior through the enforcement (or non-enforcement) of antidiscrimination and equal opportunity policies.

The Military Leadership Diversity Commission (MLDC)[2] is invested in developing "diversity leadership" in the U.S. military because of the advantages of institutional diversity. The commission defines diversity leadership as leadership which is able to overcome the differences among service members and get everyone working toward the same goals so that the increased innovation, creativity, and differences in perspective and skills associated with diversity can be effectively utilized. When diversity is left unmanaged, existing social categorizations can overpower the shared military aims and lead to splintering. According to the MLDC, successful diversity leadership has more to do with having a specific perspective—consideration of how diversity affects the mission—than with specific leadership practices. However, they provide some broad guidance for leadership invested in diversity. Leaders who value diversity will instill a sense of identity based on mission rather than other social categories and will actively manage diversity to avoid the formation of identities based on social rather than military characteristics. This involves leaders being proactive in managing diversity-related conflicts and being fair in their use of rewards and punishments. They must both model inclusion and enforce formal policies. Another element of good diversity leadership is facilitating effective communication. Effective leaders must learn how to communicate with subordinates who may have a different perspective. Successful diversity leaders must also learn to operate beyond assumptions and stereotypes. In order to effectively leverage diversity, leadership also must provide the tools to do the job. A lack of resources can lead to the disintegration of cohesion as individuals default to existing divisions in the scramble for scarce resources or rewards or to avoid punishment. Finally, leadership must establish personal and professional credibility.

Leadership that valued diversity and was invested in providing a supportive environment tended to lead to positive experiences for the people who spoke with me. For those respondents who experienced adversity as a consequence of being Muslim, leadership often played a central role in exacerbating tensions. In addition to controlling rewards and punishments, leaders also set the tone for the unit. Leaders communicate through their actions and attitudes what behaviors are expected and acceptable.

In this chapter, I present two cases of leadership that valued and supported diversity, though examples of this type of leadership can also be found throughout this book. I also present two cases where weak leadership, or leadership that exacerbates existing tensions, negatively shaped the experiences of Muslim service members.

TAREK: COHESION IN THE CLINIC

Tarek is a veteran who worked in a stateside military clinic for four years where he served military service members and their families. Born in South Asia, Tarek came to the United States as a child. He was primarily motivated to join the military by the benefits, such as money for college and on-the-job medical training. He also voiced a desire to serve as a way of giving back:

> So many people come into this country and don't do anything to, like all
> they do is take; no one gives back. Honestly I didn't do it because I had this

epiphany of patriotism but I did it to better myself, but then once I joined, after being in the military, I found a sense of pride, it sounds very clichéd but [. . .] I had that.

Tarek was the first in his immediate family to serve in the military, though he had an uncle and a cousin who served in the U.S. military. His mother was concerned about his decision to join the military because of the ongoing conflicts in Iraq and Afghanistan, but his father approved of the decision, seeing it as a good long-term investment.

My father wanted me to do it just because at the time financially we weren't doing very well and I didn't really apply myself in high school. He wasn't 100 percent about me going, but he felt long term it would be good for me. My mother at the time didn't want me to go because we still have a strong presence in Iraq and Afghanistan, so of course they were worried.

In our conversations, Tarek brought up some of the social pressures he and his family felt within their ethnic and religious community.

My parents were affected a lot by people in the community, [. . .] like the Muslim community or even neighbors were very concerned like "Oh this is your only son, have you sent him off to war?"

While he felt supported by the outpouring of community concern for his well-being, Tarek quickly grew tired of having to explain why he was making the choice to join the military. He characterized much of this resistance as being a product of ignorance about the U.S. military:

Most people don't know anything in regards to what each branch does, the military has so many components, it's not [always] somebody with a gun. First thing they think of the military is an Army soldier or Marine, some people didn't understand that [I] went to the medical community. [. . .] Even after I got out [. . .], people were still like "Oh, they let you go." They thought it was a prison sentence, that's the feeling I got. [. . .] They thought that I was brainwashed or something like that.

Similar to Kareem, Tarek also explained this reluctance of the community to fully embrace his military service as a product of cultural expectations, which he was violating.

But especially in the community that I was in, [. . .] basically you come to this country to try to advance yourself, and if you're not a doctor or lawyer or an engineer you're considered a failure. Now it's become easier and easier for people [. . .] to accept other trades, but I know it didn't sit well with a lot of people because no one has an idea that there's something else besides college. [. . .] I didn't fault them for that, I didn't have a sense of resentment, I just carried on.

Tarek was proud of his military service. Although he began with a joke, the depth of his pride was clear:

[I: Are you proud to be a veteran?] Oh yeah. I get to eat free at Applebee's, it's great [laughs]. [. . .] It's nice, the country as a whole always has pride and respect for people who served. I'm not trying to milk it or anything but it is nice, you have more pride than you had before, everyday it kinda grows. So it's nice.

Tarek enjoyed the military lifestyle:

I liked the discipline of it, all those different things that I didn't like at the time, like I didn't like being told what to do, but at the end of the day the military is a cakewalk compared to jobs in the real world.

Now that he is out, Tarek appreciates some of the differences between civilian work and military service. "I don't have a chain of command any more, I just have a HR department and an immediate supervisor. That's it. So that kinda freedom is nice [. . .] I get to grow my hair out."

In a familiar theme, Tarek saw his military service as a series of opportunities, especially for education and travel.

I started to realize that there's opportunity for education, there's opportunity for advancement, there's opportunity to travel; it's a very accommodating environment if you allow it. People tend to think that the military is harsh and is no room to grow and I never had that feeling. I enjoyed being around other service members. So in a nutshell I enjoyed the variety of it.

He also saw the military as providing the opportunity to broaden his own horizons while recognizing, in line with the contact hypothesis, that as a South Asian Muslim American, he was broadening the horizons of some of his colleagues.

I think a lot of times when people join the military they go outside their bubble just like I did. But it was easier for me to get used to it because I grew up in a diverse part of the country. I know there's kids I went to boot camp with that never saw snow and I know there are kids I went to boot camp with, I know this one kid from Kentucky he never saw an African American, you know he never saw me, a brown person. There's still people like that in this country and that's ok. It just comes down to how you deal with your experiences.

When I asked him if he would make the same decision to join the military again, he was sure he would. "I would. I wouldn't change my job or anything like that." He valued his own military service but recognized it may not be for everyone.

I always think if I had a kid or something like that I wouldn't force him or her to serve, but it really comes down to your situation. [. . .] It's always a different situation why someone joined whether they're Muslim or not: school, patriotism, you name it.

Tarek and I spoke a while after Nidal Hassan attacked fellow soldiers at Fort Hood, killing thirteen people. Tarek shared his reaction to the Fort Hood shooting:

When I heard about it I was at work, and it's not like I was looking over my shoulder or anything but I think people around me were objective enough to realize, ok, this guy has more things going on than being Muslim. He was also disturbed and angry and frustrated [. . .] I guess that's just my way of thinking that it's just like Timothy McVeigh and the guys at Columbine, it's a common theme, someone is emotionally disturbed. I talk to people and they ask me "Hey, what do you think?" And I'm like he deserves the worst penalty. It's a shame because he was supposed to be the one consoling people, that's the thing that frustrates me, 'cause not only am I Muslim, but I'm in the medical community. It was like a double, triple hit for me.

Tarek was a practicing Muslim who, among other things, only ate halal[3] meat.

During boot camp all the meat wasn't halal so I was basically vegetarian, so I lost a lot of weight. I got in shape so it was an advantage.

When we talked about whether he worked with other Muslim service members, he explained that it varied from base to base. On the smaller bases he often did not know of any other Muslims; but he told me that larger bases had active

Muslim populations, with some offering Friday prayers on base. He would attend these prayers when he was there, otherwise, he would try to go to a local civilian mosque. Tarek still lives in an area near a military base and sees this reflected at his local mosque: "You'll see a lot of guys who pray while wearing their uniform because they just got off work, or they've got to go back to work." He characterized that as being usual for the area and not a cause of much controversy at the mosque, explaining that his veteran status might "spark up a conversation but nothing that's crazy." He explains to me that he thinks that mosques with a longer history in the community tend to be more open and accepting to the varied occupational choices their worshippers make.

> They tend to have members who are educated, members that are involved in the community, that are involved in politics, like the councilman for my district here, he's Muslim. [. . .] So little by little, more by more I think the emphasis is to become more involved in this country.

Due to his work schedule, fasting during Ramadan did not require any accommodation, though he did discover how much he had previously been relying on the support of his family in maintaining the fast.

> [I] just did my 9 to 5, it was fine. It's hard to do it solo, I didn't realize. That was the tough part because when I was growing up, mom would wake us all up, we'd crawl out of bed, stuff food in our face, pray, and then go back to sleep. On my own it was all on me so of course it was tough, there were times when I wouldn't eat in the morning and fast without, but you just get it done, just a part of being an adult I guess.

Tarek thought that he was largely identified by others as being Muslim due to his name and his appearance.

> I have a very common [Muslim] name, very popular name, and obviously the way I look. So most people are like where are you from? Well, I was born in South Asia but I grew up in New Jersey, and the first thing people say, it still surprises, it's still pretty funny, they're like "Wow you don't have an accent." They associate South Asian people with the guy from *The Simpsons*.[4] I came here with my family when I was five years old. I don't think people get that.

Although he did witness anti-Muslim comments from other service members, Tarek did not report feeling targeted or treated in a discriminatory manner.

There's times where you feel uncomfortable, but I think a lot of that was associated with people making remarks, the same type of prejudice, certain opinions that you get with people who weren't in the military. For example, someone making a remark about terrorists or someone making a remark about al-Qaeda. All those negative things you hear on the news. It was never targeted toward me. I was always [a] peer; side by side.

Tarek did talk about one particular situation where a patient had a negative interaction with him based on his identity as a Muslim. However, the event led to an increased sense of inclusion when his colleagues and superior rallied around him, demonstrating the role of strong leadership in shaping the unit environment. On this occasion, Tarek was working at night in the clinic when a family came in with a sick child.

I did have one patient be a little racist towards me. But the surprising thing was I just brushed it off. I was working in the pediatric clinic and I was checking in this lady's daughter. And she looked at my name badge, she was friendly, she wasn't angry towards me at all, and she's like "Oh are you Muslim?" So I said "Yeah I am." I didn't hesitate, I said it with pride. And she was like "How radical are you?" And I was taken aback because it is very shocking. And I just said, "I'm not radical at all." And I just ignored her.

In this situation, the patient presumably identified Tarek as "other" because of his name (perhaps in combination with his appearance). She then made a comment that reflected a stereotyped belief that all Muslims are inherently "radical." Shocked, Tarek ignored the incident until his superior addressed it with him later.

The doctor I was working with was right next door and she heard the conversation, so we were closing up the clinic and she was like "Wow I'm really impressed how you handled that." And I said, "What do you mean?" And she said, "I would have been furious."

The doctor, one of Tarek's superiors, offered Tarek support, both informally by congratulating him for handling the situation well and also formally by suggesting that a formal grievance be filed. Tarek felt that this would only exacerbate the situation.

My clinic manager wanted to file a grievance against this patient. I was like "Whoa, time out." The last thing I want is this lady's kids to hate me because they can't go see their pediatrician. And I thought about it and everybody at work was like comforting me and they were like "Wow, I can't believe she said that." But I think it was just she chose her words very poorly and it's a shame [. . .] I didn't lose faith in people, I actually gained faith in people because all of my coworkers [were] comforting me and supporting me, that was nice.

By providing support to Tarek, and respecting his decision to drop the matter, Tarek's superior modeled a commitment to maintaining a supportive workplace. Tarek's coworkers expressed their support of him after the incident, demonstrating the cohesion of this work unit. The support of his coworkers contextualized the stereotypes of one patient as a minority opinion, allowing Tarek to largely dismiss the incident. In focusing on the task of effectively providing health care to military families, the staff of the clinic drew together, supporting each other.

ZAFIR: FEELING UNDER ATTACK

Zafir was one of the first people I spoke with for this project. We met at a café and Zafir told me about his four years in the military. He and his family immigrated to the United States from South Asia when he was an adult. He joined the military with dreams of using his language and culture skills to help the U.S. military, but found himself entangled in unit-level politics. He felt that he was singled out for negative treatment because of his religious identity. Feeling disgusted with the system, he left the military.

As was common with the people who spoke with me, Zafir saw a sense of service as being one of his main motivations for joining the military:

I wanted to do *my* part to serve the country and to utilize my knowledge, my skills and abilities about Middle Eastern and South Asian cultures [and] languages so I actually joined the military.

For Zafir and his family, military service was associated with ideas of heroism and patriotism:

My mom felt pretty good because she knew that her son was gonna be a hero. She loved the United States.

As we talked, Zafir spoke at length about why he thought it is crucial to maintain a diverse military. In this view, having practicing Muslim service members in the U.S. military served as proof of religious tolerance in the United States and demonstrated that the current operations target terrorism, not Islam. Zafir argued:

I think I should work here so that I can stop people like Osama bin Laden and people of al-Qaeda and Taliban in their propaganda that the United States is fighting a war against Islam and Muslims.

He also argued fervently that inclusion is an important tool against radicalism:

It's very important to impose the [Equal Opportunity] policies and to make sure that those Muslims who are serving in the military are not called Taliban or al-Qaeda, like I was [. . .] We have to learn from previous experiences. I gave them an example of the 7/7 bombing in London.[5] I told them that those people who committed that act they were born in the United Kingdom, [. . .] and the terrorism experts [think] that most probably [they] were suffering from identity crisis because [they were] born and raised there and they have a feeling in general that they are not treated like the white British people. So it becomes easy for the radicals to recruit them and tell them, "Hey, these people hate you because you're a Muslim," so they go against their own country. My fear is that this may happen in the military. If they don't control and impose the EO policies we may end up seeing something like 7/7. And the fear came true when I heard about the Fort Hood shooting and the person who did it he said that he was discriminated against.

Zafir continued by comparing the exclusionary attitudes he experienced to the willingness of al-Qaeda to accept followers based on ideology rather than ethnicity or background.

[I was] helping the United States with the education I got, not because I wanted to get something but to do my part to serve the country. How was [the] United States gonna win the war against an enemy who doesn't care about the skin color, about the country of national origin, about the English accent of a California-born white American, Adam Gadahn or John Walker [Lindh], and [Richard] Reid.[6] Because those people they, even though they are evil people, but they are very sincere to their cause. And I was not finding a lot of sincerity with the people I was working with.

For Zafir, trying to fight an enemy that is willing and able to make use of diverse forces requires that the U.S. military learn how to effectively include diverse service members in its forces.

Zafir worked in a language and culture specialty and found that he had to begin by educating those he worked with on the very basics of the region. He spoke about encountering a conflation of different populations, probably based on common stereotypes that treat Islam and the Middle East and South Asia as monolithic.

> Like they thought that Afghanistan was an Arab country. I was the first person who told them that it's not an Arab country. Was it a Middle Eastern country? I said No, it's actually a South Asian country.

Later in our discussion he recalled having to explain to his colleagues that different languages were spoken throughout Pakistan.

After talking for a bit about his background and his early days in the military, Zafir began to tell me about his experience working for a specific commander. He felt that this commander consistently treated him poorly because of Zafir's identity:

> The most negative experience, I felt, was the mindset of the people. [. . .] They do their best to punish that person in order to remind him that if he doesn't belong to their race, or their skin color, or their life as a child he is wrong.

He listed the mistreatments he perceived, which included disadvantageous treatment in duty assignment, projects that wasted his skills, and accusations of misconduct and disloyalty. Zafir told me that this commander also called him names:

> [My commander] once called me a Taliban and once he told me that I was trying to infiltrate the military.

Zafir also felt that his commander was actively targeting him for negative treatment. In addition to name calling, Zafir reported that he was regularly ordered to take on tasks outside his duties, including babysitting and assembling furniture.

> [My commander] was trying to do something so that I get frustrated and I disrespect him. I didn't do it. He told me to make shelves, I made them, even though they were not related to [my job] at all.

Subsequently, Zafir told me, he was accused by a coworker of sexual harassment:

> She started flirting with me. [. . .] So I started flirting back. And then she introduced me to another female, and they both were flirting with me. Then

one day I got a call from my first sergeant in the unit. She said that "somebody filed a sexual harassment complaint against you."

The complaint was taken to a higher jurisdiction and Zafir was required to appear before a board where charges of disloyalty were added:

I was shocked to hear what they say. They said that this guy, he was flirting with us and not only this, but he came to us and told us that he didn't get deployed, that I didn't get deployed because I support the insurgents.

Eventually, Zafir told me, the accusations of disloyalty were dropped, though he continued to pursue the matter:

I actually filed a complaint against those females, that what they made was a false accusation.

Zafir presented his complaints to a colonel who tried to mollify him:

When I appeared before a full-bird colonel, he told me "Ok, forget all these things, tell me what *I* can do for *you*." [. . .] He told me that a majority of people in the United States are so ignorant, we go to France, Germany and talk to them in English expecting they be able to speak English, so he said that this is a problem in our country, people are ignorant. It's not ignorance. False accusations were made, it was preplanned.

Despite the apparent support of some elements of the command structure, Zafir told me that problems remained with his immediate commander. Zafir also told me that this particular leader had a history of problematic encounters with nonwhite soldiers.

One time he actually verbally abused the security personnel in the garage because they were African Americans [. . .] And he had a weird excuse all the time, he used to tell me that he was white and he worked at [redacted] which is predominately black and he was always discriminated [against]. So I said, "Sir, I wasn't the person who was discriminating against you, why should you discriminate against me?"

This suggests that this particular commander may have been what leadership experts George Reed and R. Craig Bullis call a "destructive leader."[7] At the very least, this was a leader who was uninterested in supporting diversity. In this situation, Zafir's treatment may have had more to do with the general prejudices of this leader than with Zafir's Muslim identity; that is, if Zafir had been nonwhite but Christian, he might still have been singled out for negative treatment, as the guards in the garage allegedly were. However, that the reported mistreatment took the form it did reflects the post-9/11 environment—in another historical moment it is unlikely he would have been called "Taliban" or accused of disloyalty.

For Zafir, the final straw came when he felt his family was being dragged into the conflict. At the time he lived with his mother. After the charges against Zafir were dismissed, he told me that his commander made repeated demands that Zafir and his mother host him at their home.

> The worst thing that happened was that he insisted [I] tell my family members to invite him at my home. I told my mother, my mother says, "That sounds kinda weird, why should we invite him?" And he was continuously insisting [. . .] And I said, "If it was my home I could invite you, my mom is not ready for this." And he said, "Do you live at your mother's home or your mother lives at your home?" I said, "She's my mother, I'm her son, it doesn't matter who lives at whose home and who's paying the money." [. . .] He said, "No you have to invite me." I said, "Ok, I can try. I will ask my mother. If she [agrees] that's okay." And he did it seven times. [. . .] My mother was so frustrated. She was so angry. She said that he is treating us like slaves because my mother doesn't fall under the chain of command, I'm the person who falls under the chain of command. [. . .] He told me that it was never an order, but he told me that you gotta do it.

Zafir eventually enlisted the help of the Equal Opportunity (EO) office. Ultimately his commander was ordered to stop this behavior, though Zafir was angry as he told me that his commander was subsequently relocated and then promoted.

> I found out that that captain who mistreated me, mistreated my family members [. . .] was promoted in rank from captain to major just after that formal complaint in which they acknowledged the fact that what he did by harassing my family members were wrong, they said that he was gonna take the cultural classes. I said it's not a cultural issue, it's a human rights issue.

Zafir's negative experiences took a toll on his health:

I got so frustrated at that time, I got so sick I couldn't sleep for three days, I went to the hospital; they gave me medication. That was the first time that happened to me that I experienced insomnia and it was terrible.

Zafir told me that he decided to leave the military due to these experiences and the opinions of his mother and wife.

When I joined the military I had so many things in my mind that I would help the United States. [. . .] So I wanted to utilize those things but all my time was wasted in proving myself right and refuting other people's false accusation. [. . .] So I mean this was really frustrating, and so after that I actually had no choice but because of my family pressure I [left the] military.

Zafir was one of the few people I spoke with who reported extremely negative experiences. Throughout his service he felt that he was treated unfairly and that his unique skills and knowledge were wasted. Ultimately this led him to leave the military and left a very negative impression of military service with him and his family. Many of Zafir's negative experiences stemmed from interactions with a particular leader whom Zafir notes might have been generally prejudiced against racial and ethnic minorities. This leader himself created problems for Zafir, but also fostered a culture of suspicion in the unit.

NAJIB: ACCOMMODATION AT AN ACADEMY

When we spoke, Najib was currently serving in the military, and had been for nine years. It took a while to arrange a time to speak with Najib because he was stationed overseas, and coordinating work schedules and the time difference was challenging. Najib graduated from a service academy, and when we spoke he was working in a support position. Najib's parents emigrated from South Asia, and he was born in the United States.

Najib decided to apply for a service academy after not getting onto the prestigious civilian academic track he desired:

I wanted to go to a magnet [high] school and I failed [. . .] I was like what am I going to do with my life if I can't get into a magnet school and go to Harvard or MIT and be a scientist or whatever. And then I somehow learned about the Academy and I saw all the opportunities that there was coming out of the Academy.

He also connects his motivations to popular media:

> When I was little I played too many computer games, it was a flight simulation that sparked a little bit of interest, and then I read too many Tom Clancy books which sparked a little bit more interest and then I wanted to [join the military].

Najib characterizes his parents' reaction to his decision to join the military as being negative: "They were really against it." Like the parents of Kareem and Tarek, Najib's family viewed his decision to join the military as a deviation from their expectations. He describes his family's move to the United States as being a familiar story for South Asian immigrants. His father excelled academically:

> He was first in his class in his village, [. . .] graduated with a master's degree and became a lecturer. He wanted to move on and gain higher status in the university, to be a professor. In order to do that he had to get a master's or PhD from a foreign university. [. . .] You have to go to the West [. . .] to get that degree, then you can come back and teach.

His father studied in the United States for two years, then Najib's mother and older siblings joined him. Four years after leaving home, Najib's father got his degree and the family decided to stay in the United States. "My mom convinced him that [. . .] we're here now, this is the best opportunity for the kids, the best opportunity for us, so we might as well stay because if we go back home there's nothing there for you." Najib was born in the United States. Najib's older siblings followed in the academic footsteps of their father.

> My brothers majored in engineering and my sister majored in neuroscience, and they all have decent careers in their fields, and here I am doing something completely off the ball, joining the service, and potentially going to war, and not coming home. So they were really against it.

His family also had concerns about his safety:

> They were really against [me joining the military]. They said if you do this with the world in this kind of state, we're afraid what's going to happen, [. . .] you're going to get hurt.

Ultimately they accepted his decision. He noted, however, that his family would still prefer he resume the expected life course:

They still want me eventually to leave, like as soon as possible. "Eventually as soon as possible," makes sense, right? But that's more because they want me to get on with my life and start a family, get married, have kids, the things that they were raised to do. As South Asian guys, we're supposed to go to school, get an education, get a job, get married, have kids, have a family. And so far I've got an education and I've got a job, so [I'm] a little behind the curve.

Najib enjoyed his military service and (in a common theme) saw the opportunities presented by the military as a major appeal. He described what made the military a positive experience for him:

the opportunity to meet so many different kinds of people all over the world and the ability to work with such high-caliber people [. . .]. And there's the camaraderie. I don't know what it's like to work in the civilian world, but they say it's not like that in the civilian world. The level of professionalism in my experience in the military, you just can't beat it, and I really appreciate that.

He also appreciated the opportunities for travel:

I'm meeting people from all over the world. [. . .] [It's] really cool 'cause I'm meeting all different kinds of cultures [. . .] There's a difference between tourists and travelers. Tourists are like people on vacation; travelers are also on vacation, but they're actually learning and experiencing and talking to people and stuff. I had a taste of traveling [. . .] I had the opportunity here and *inshAllah* [God willing] I will continue to travel after I leave the military.

Najib also acknowledged the benefits of the job and the accompanying financial stability, though he refers to this as "lesser" than the other benefits:

freedom from financial hardship because you have a steady income. I can afford a house, [. . .] I was twenty-five and I bought my first house [. . .] I'm doing well in that respect.

When I asked him if he'd do it all over again he responded, "I wouldn't do it again, but I wouldn't have done anything else. I guess I'm glad I chose the path that I took."

Najib did not think that being Muslim had affected his military career:

Maybe I'm naive, but I don't think people look at me as a Muslim, I think they just look at me as another guy in the office.

He told me that discussions of religion rarely came up within his unit:

> If it was a topic of conversation it was a topic of conversation when we had free time, and we didn't have a whole lot of time, we were mostly working. I don't think that people were afraid to talk about it, I think it just didn't matter at the time, in that environment.

Najib's descriptions of his experiences add to the evidence that in a healthy unit—one that is not plagued by rumor, gossip, and suspicion—normal processes of cohesion are more than able to incorporate Muslim service members, making them just another member of the team.

When I asked Najib if his colleagues knew he was Muslim he said they did: "If they ask I'm going to tell them. I have no reason to hide it from them." Najib describes his religious practice as "off and on." "I don't practice very much. It kinda goes off and on. I fall off the horse and get back on the train, or whatever the expression is." During his service, his level of communal practice has varied depending on accessibility. At some postings he found that the closest community was too far away to attend regularly.

> Basically the closer [geographically] I am to a community the more involved I'm gonna be with the community and the activities and the closer I'm gonna become to the religion. [. . .] So for me the religion is much stronger when I'm with a community because I like the people in the community, they're just good human beings and I feel a connection with them and with my own faith when I'm near them. But when I'm not around them, like when I'm on deployment, [. . .] or something where I'm not here, then I don't feel that connection as much.

Najib has considered taking on leadership roles in several local civilian communities, but has ultimately declined because his military career requires that he move frequently.

At his current posting, Najib only knew of one other Muslim service member. "I'm sure there are others, I've just only met one."

As a former cadet at one of the academies, Najib also provided a window into institutionalized religious accommodation. Najib discussed requesting time to attend Friday prayers. Usually these accommodations went smoothly, though he recalls one year when the academy rabbi had to get involved to convince a new leader that the Muslim cadets should be granted permission to leave base to attend Eid[8] services in the civilian community.

We had someone in our leadership who didn't understand why we needed to leave the academy to go for the Eid, Eid al-Fitr, right after Ramadan. [He thought we should] just hold our own service on base, [. . .] There were sixteen students and we wanted to go to a mosque and have a proper Eid, with the prayer and the celebration and everything. He just didn't understand why we needed to do that. But the rabbi was very supportive of us and he set us up with the permission needed to go off base to do that. [. . .] So until the night before the holiday we weren't sure if we'd be able to leave the base because our leadership was so averse to us leaving base and missing out on a day of classes to go to our worship, but *ilhumdallah* [thank God] it came through and we took the day off.

Najib also told me about how at the academy there were institutional preparations for Ramadan which enabled Muslim cadets to fast with a minimum of fuss or disruption.

So at the academy they know that it's coming; they prepare for it and are ready. The Food Service Officers have the guys prepare like a box lunch. [. . .] And so we get that for breakfast. So we wake up in the middle of the night and eat and say our prayers. [. . .] When the Muslims all had dinner [during Ramadan] at the academy we went to a separate room in the dining area and we ate dinner together, the same dinner as everyone else, we just didn't have pork served to us. It was a good time. And then they also have those boxed lunches for morning there so we just take them to our rooms and we could eat it in our rooms in the morning.

Najib found that this institutional support shaped his religious practice. Accommodation being provided as a part of everyday life at the academy encouraged his observation of the fast. After leaving the academy, seeking religious accommodation and making preparations for the fast fell upon him as an individual and he was more likely to forgo the practice. "After the academy it was completely on us and there were years when I just didn't fast." This is an interesting example of how much difference normalized institutional support can make.

The accommodations made by the academy were also a tangible way to support diversity. By taking the initiative in providing boxed breakfasts for fasting cadets and providing a space for them to break their fast at the end of the day, the academy was communicating that this diversity is valued. Cadets who wanted to fast could easily do so without having to worry about formally requesting accommodation from the leadership who had an unknown attitude toward Islam.

After leaving the academy Najib had some mixed experiences, but eventually he landed a position with a commander whom he deeply respected. As we spoke about this experience, Najib told me about how having strong leadership creates a sense of self-worth and positivity:

> The most proud thing that I can feel was knowing that our boss and the guys in command trusted us to do the jobs that we were doing, that we are sometimes the only guys that could do the job that we were doing. That's a good feeling when your boss trusts you to do something, to go out on your own and do that, that's something that's very important.

Najib also talked about how his commander went out of his way to show respect and interest in Middle Eastern culture. At the time, Najib was serving in a Middle Eastern country (outside the war zone) and his commander, a non-Arab and a non-Muslim, made a conscious effort to learn about and respect the local culture, which had positive effects in building rapport locally, and also gave Najib a sense of pride in this leader.

> [My superior's] speech is very eloquent, he's very well versed [. . .] [My commander and some locals] have conversations about Islam pretty regularly. He's very curious about it and he knows quite a bit, and he's learning Arabic a little bit, he practiced Arabic in his office and his kids are taking Arabic. His son is actually pretty good. So he comes from a very open-minded family I think. It's kind of refreshing to have that personality that you're working with every day.

This superior's interest in the local culture has become a bit of a joke in their unit. Earlier in our conversation I had used the phrase *inshAllah*, an expression meaning "God willing" that is commonly used when talking about the future, and Najib had laughed; he explained why:

> It was really funny when you said *inshAllah* because he [my superior] says that all the time [laughs]. He told me the other day, "You know, I probably say *inshAllah* more often than I should and I think it's getting to people around here." But it's kinda funny for him, the way he says it and as often as he uses it, "Well, we'll do this if this happens *inshAllah*" [laughs]. So nonchalantly it just comes out of him naturally.

This normalization of cultural competence, the idea that even an officer in a leadership position would make the effort to learn another language and culture, speaks volumes to the unit about the value of respecting and striving to understand the local culture. Interestingly, this level of everyday respect occurred here in a unit that did not have a primary mission relating to language, culture, or intelligence.

BASIM: ACCOMMODATION DENIED

Another example of the role of leadership in shaping the environment and acceptance of Muslim service members was the experiences of Basim. Basim is a veteran who spent over twenty years as a linguist for the military. He served in both Afghanistan and Iraq. Basim joined the military due to difficulties finding stable employment. Although he enjoyed most of his career, Basim told me that after 9/11 the atmosphere changed. Upset with institutionalized suspicion in his unit and difficulties getting religious accommodation, he decided to retire.

Basim had immigrated to the United States from the Middle East as a teenager in order to pursue his education. Unable to find steady employment, Basim decided that the military was his best option:

I didn't have a job and I work[ed] from fast food restaurant to fast food restaurant and nobody [was] hiring, almost like we have now. Then I decided to go ahead and join the military. At least there was something stable. [. . .] I was living on my own, trying to make rent and the car payments and everything else and I was struggling, so finally I joined the military and it worked out for me.

Basim's family was generally accepting of his decision to join the military and he enjoyed the majority of his career. Talking about what it's like being out of the military, he explained some of what made him like his time in the military:

I miss the military. I miss the camaraderie, the people, the unit togetherness and everything else. Outside everybody [is] for themselves, they worry about themselves. And in the military, everybody, no matter what, they still take care of [each other].

Basim is a devout Muslim. "Everybody knows I'm Muslim because I practice my religion. I fast in Ramadan, I pray five times a day, I go to the Friday prayer." While Basim was open about being Muslim, he recognized that others might be uncomfortable with this. "I know a lot of Muslims who maybe put 'Other' on their religion. When they ask them what's your religion, "Oh, I don't have one." So they just wouldn't check 'Muslim.'"

For most of his career, Basim had no issues getting accommodations that allowed him to maintain this level of practice. He described his usual experience attending Friday prayers:

> I always request that I can go [to] Friday prayer and make sure I work extra when I come back. Instead of taking time off, I take my lunch hour, but since the mosque is about fifteen minutes and fifteen minutes back, I always told them I'll work extra time, for each minute I'll work two minutes. So if I'm late by fifteen minutes I'll go ahead and put in half an hour. They were always understanding.

Basim had the experience of working at a base with a large enough Muslim population to hold regular Friday prayers on the installation. He described the security situation surrounding these gatherings, explaining that attendees were required to show military identification and that all civilians (primarily civilians working on the base) had to be escorted by a military member. Arrangements for the large Eid service required advanced planning.

> So they put a barricade before the mosque and start asking people for their ID and we have to vouch for them [civilians], even though some of them worked for the Department of Defense. They'd call me, "I'm here at the gate." I'd say "He's ok, he's with me." Then at the Eid, after Ramadan, I had to submit the names in advance so they can check them out or look at them or something, the people who were coming to pray with us, the congregation prayer, it's like once a year or twice a year, so we have to submit their names to the security.

As we talked, Basim made it clear that the majority of his time in the military was positive. He connected his positive perception of most of his service with the quality of leaders he served under:

> I think the whole military experience was positive for me. I had the best officers; they allowed me to do my job, allowed me to pray. [. . .] I think out of probably twenty or more officers, every one of them [except one] was outstanding. The one guy, he was really bad, and we had a lot of friction and I ended up leaving the unit because of that [. . .] But other than that, one out of twenty, I always thank God for that. The majority was positive.

Before 9/11, his service made him feel like a part of something bigger, a part of the nation. But the suspicion with which he was treated following 9/11 eroded this sense of belonging. For Basim, 9/11 was a defining moment in his military career. Up until this point he had enjoyed his military service, and he intended to stay not just to retirement at twenty years, but for a full thirty years. However, in his view, 9/11 changed the way he was perceived and treated:

> I'm proud to be a veteran. It was a good life, it was a good experience, and I'll never forget it, even with the negative at the end of it, you can't expect life to go by with everything good in it. Bad and good.

Basim told me that following 9/11 he was treated with suspicion and he was even asked to report to the base security office where he was questioned. As he related this experience, I could hear the frustration in his voice as he talked about feeling suddenly singled out. He seemed particularly affronted by the temerity of questioning his loyalty in the face of his two decades of service.

> It wasn't bad 'til September 11th, then they start looking at us different. Generalizing everybody. Even the people who you care for and work with and know you all this time, they start looking at you in a different way, like suspicious. I noticed that a lot of times it seemed like we were watched, we were asked to report to the [security office] and they question us: what's your life, who you know, who you don't know, what do you know. A lot of things that make you feel like you're not part of the unit, not part of the [military]. I contacted other Muslims and they say they went through the same thing and that's why I was really upset then because I'd been in the military for almost twenty years, and some guy just been in the military for three years he questioned my integrity and my patriotism asking me question like that: do you know what is a sleeper cell? I'm familiar with that, I'm military, we study it. [. . .] So then I retired [. . .] because of the treatment. Prior to September 11th everything was outstanding, you feel like you're part of the country, part of the military, you're doing your job, you're doing your part, everybody like an intricate machine. Then on September 11th they start looking at us in a different light, even though they know me for almost twenty years, know my work, my integrity, everything I do for the country, and they start putting you in a questionable place.

Despite the negative treatment, Basim told me he did find support among his colleagues:

But a lot of the people I worked with who've known me all these years, they stood up with me and they were ready to do anything possible to stop the interrogation and stop the questioning.

His long career prior to 9/11 may have contributed to a breakdown of prejudice through extended contact. Colleagues who had worked with him were less likely to accept the suspicion of him; their personal knowledge of him trumped stereotypes about the untrustworthiness of Muslims.

Although Basim felt that the whole military atmosphere changed following 9/11, it was a change in leadership and the denial of the religious accommodation that he was accustomed to that was the final straw. Having been granted permission to leave work to pray, especially to attend congregational prayers on Friday afternoons, throughout his career, Basim was shocked when a new commander denied his request.

[My commander] said "No, I can't let you go to Friday prayer, and I can't allow you to do this and do that," so I continued praying but I had to hide it. I pray whenever he goes somewhere, I pray when he's not around [. . .] I felt like I'm not even a human being if you can prevent me from praying, and I had to hide myself behind the curtains just to do the prayer. I felt like this is not America, this is not the country I came to, the country I love, the country I respect and [it] made me have a negative tone about the whole thing. I mean it's not right. But I can't do anything because everybody's looking at us in a different light now.

More than just seeking privacy, Basim recounted having to literally hide himself in order to pray. For Basim, being denied the right to pray was a blow against his sense of belonging. These experiences directly influenced his decision to leave the military.

I was planning on staying to the end, 'till almost thirty years, whatever I can stay. Like I said, people who come in new, three years in, because of their job with the [security office] asking you about your integrity. [. . .] It's not right, it's not what I expected from the military. Even though I love it so much, and I still do.

Basim was unsure how much of his experiences to share with his children, who he hopes will not experience the same sense of exclusion he did.

My son now is in ROTC, at first I didn't want to tell him; I don't want to tell him not to join, not to do that, [. . .] because he was born here, he lived here all his life, maybe [his experiences] gonna be different than mine, I don't want to influence him. [. . .] To stress the negative is not a good thing. I want him to live his life without being influenced by my experience, especially in something like that. He might find it a lot better.

Despite his negative experiences at the end of his service, after leaving the military Basim recognized that the military provided a level of protection absent in civilian society.

It's a big-time adjustment. Just like going from a controlled area, a fishbowl, to an open sea where you can be a target to anybody and you can't do anything about it. [If] anybody in the military called me names I would just go to unit commander and he would reprimand them. Here people scream at you in the streets, calling you names, but you can't do anything about it. If you call the police and say, "Hey this guy called me names." "Well we can't do anything about it unless he threatened your life." And that's an adjustment, yes. [. . .] It was hard for the first couple of years, and now I've adjusted to the people around you here, you know, say things to you. In the military nobody ever called you a "sandnigger" or anything, but here my kids in school, they are called names.

Basim was hopeful for his children's future as Americans even as he expressed some concerns. He explained that his mother used to live in the United States but got tired of hearing "a lot of negative comments" because she dressed "traditionally." She returned to the Middle East. Basim explains, "She [doesn't] want to come back after she experienced what she did. She used to love America, to love the people. But now she says she does not, and she worries about us more than ever."

Basim described a situation where a change in leadership had dramatic effects on his experiences. After two decades of service in which his identity as a practicing Muslim had little effect on his experiences, a new commander and post-9/11 tensions led Basim to feel that he was being unjustly targeted for questioning and surveillance. He took this as a personal affront given his long and loyal service. When his new commander denied him the religious accommodation he was accustomed to having, Basim decided it was time to leave the military.

FIVE

THE ROLE OF DIVERSITY

The military structure and an emphasis on equal opportunity contributed to positive experiences for several of the people who spoke with me. Strong leadership also facilitated feelings of being included, while weak leadership shaped atmospheres of divisiveness within other units. Strong leadership is more likely when leaders recognize the importance of diversity and see it as a resource that can help them achieve their mission. In this chapter, I'll share two stories where diversity was not fully utilized, and two stories where diversity was used proactively.

OMAR: LANGUAGES AND SUSPICION

When I spoke with Omar, he had recently left the military after putting in eight years. Omar is multiracial and was born in the United States to immigrant parents. He converted to Islam while in the military.

Omar joked with me about the irony of his military service; he joined the military as an alternative to further schooling and as an opportunity to travel, but he became a linguist and spent his entire career stateside, much of it in school. He laughed as he explained:

> I just didn't want to go to college and like I didn't want to study or anything like that, and I picked like the last job for that. Like being a linguist you're constantly studying and constantly learning languages, so it kinda backfired.

Like several other people who spoke with me, Omar referenced popular media in explaining his decision to join the military:

I can understand why people want to be in the military, there's like really cool Playstation games, really cool movies. I saw *Independence Day* and I was like I gotta be in the military.

Although he decided to join the military straight out of high school, Omar—a pacifist who appreciates his independence—predictably found the military to be a mismatch for his personality and values.

My family like, they were cool with it but a lot of them didn't think I'd really do it 'cause I'm all pacifistic and stuff. So I kinda did it also to prove them like hey I'm doing this, learn how to hold a gun and stuff [laughs]. But that's why I got out though, 'cause it obviously wasn't me.

Omar was thrilled to be out of the military. While other people I spoke with talked about appreciating the discipline and hierarchy of military life, Omar found it oppressive.

I just hated the PT [physical training], all the exercise and things like that, I just want to be healthy on my own; I don't need someone telling me to be healthy. There's a lot of little nit-picky things that just add up. It's so much better being out, so much better. And not just 'cause being Muslim, it's just not a life I imagine anyone would ever want. [laughs] [. . .] I just got out and [it's] like the sun's shining, I see the flowers and everything. It's nice.

Omar converted to Islam during his military service. His process of religious exploration arose out of anti-Muslim attitudes expressed by an instructor.

In class I had this one sergeant who did a tour in Somalia, and he always had mean things to say about Muslims 'cause he was an "expert" and I didn't agree with what he said and I knew a lot of people who are Muslim—like family, relatives, or people from when I was in high school, and I had a good impression of them. I didn't know anything about it, but I knew that they were nice people. I couldn't argue with the guy because I had nothing to back up my argument, so I just went to the library and I started reading and then I liked it, and then I decided to become Muslim myself.

Growing up in a diverse community and family, Omar is an example of the contact hypothesis in the civilian context. Throughout his childhood, Omar was in contact with peers and family who were Muslim. Later in life, when Omar was confronted with stereotyped depictions of Muslims, he drew on his own experiences with Muslims that he had known to question this.

Omar's description also draws attention to the role of military education. In his unit an "expert" with a particular ideological approach was tapped to teach about Islam. This attitude does not characterize all instructors in the military, but the views expressed by particular instructors may play a role in shaping the attitudes within a unit.

For Omar, being Muslim shaped his experiences in the military in ways that he often felt were negative:

> It's always, the odds are always out of your . . . I mean even if you're Muslim and not in the military, it's still a disadvantage because everywhere you want to go for breakfast is bacon and ham and sausage. So in the military it's even more of that kind of stuff. I can't really be specific about it. But you're always on the losing end of something. You get used to it.

He felt that his identity and religious practices, such as not drinking, set him apart and prevented building strong relationships with his colleagues:

> They know that I'm not going to go drinking with them so I had less friends 'cause he's not gonna do anything cool. So they were just really good work friends and none take-home friends.

Omar's characterization of socialization with his colleagues was very different from that of Mahmood (chapter 3), who argued that although he did drink alcohol, abstaining would have had little impact on his off-duty socialization. It is possible that Mahmood's hypothesis that abstaining from alcohol would have had little effect is incorrect and that he, like Omar, would have felt excluded if he did not drink. It is more plausible, however, that other differences between Mahmood and Omar explain this discrepancy. There may be individual-level differences such as personality. There may also be unit-level differences, with Mahmood's colleagues being more accepting of abstinence than Omar's colleagues.

Omar sought formal religious accommodation during Ramadan. Rather than adapt his religious practice to his military duties, Omar adapted his military duties to accommodate fasting. Unlike many other aspects of military life, which Omar felt were weighted against him as a Muslim, accommodation for Ramadan was easy:

Whenever Ramadan came up I could just walk up to the PT leader and be like "Hey, I can't. I can't drink anything and if I run like ten seconds I'm just gonna pass out," and then he or she would just be like "Ok, just come back when it's over." And I don't think I ever really had a problem doing that.

Omar also provided an example of hiding prayer, something that several people spoke about. Omar treated prayer as a secret. Rather than explain why he would leave his office, he let his coworkers form their own ideas:

I always went somewhere isolated to pray. [. . .] There was one guy, [. . .] he was really religious, and I would meet with him to pray and we'd find some isolated place to pray. [My colleagues] probably thought we were doing something weird 'cause I'd always come in [and ask] "Are you ready?" and we'd leave every day.

Omar did feel that being Muslim had negative effects on his career, and this might also have shaped his reluctance to discuss his religious practice with his non-Muslim colleagues. He also described his colleagues as unsupportive:

They would just say all these anti-Muslim things behind my back even though they spent all day with me.

During our conversation, Omar showed me the books in several languages that cluttered his living room. One of those people with a flair for picking up new languages, Omar told me about the challenges he faced using this talent during his service. After five years working with a Romance language, Omar requested a more challenging language:

The commander said, "I will not give you an Islamic language 'cause you're Muslim." He thought I would use it to communicate with terrorists and things like that.

With the help of the Equal Opportunities Office, Omar was eventually assigned a new language, but rumors about his loyalty flourished:

After that people did have rumors about me, like maybe I would be a traitor or whatever because I was helping them with Islamic topics. [. . .] It wasn't a problem being Muslim until I started helping them out with Islamic things. For some reason that drew more attention.

Omar also alleged that within military language education, Islam was routinely excluded from the curriculum. This was also a claim made independently by Daniel, whom I will introduce next. Omar studied at the Defense Language Institute (DLI) in the early 2000s and said that at that time instructors were not allowed to teach students about Islam.

> The teachers did like me more because they weren't allowed to talk about Islam but I was because I could say I researched it and this was my project. Which I did. And the students they just loved it

Religion is a central component of culture, and its absence from a language and culture curriculum can handicap students. Learning to communicate in another language is not simply a matter of learning a new vocabulary. A whole host of nonverbal strategies must also be learned, as well as a familiarity with underlying cultural values and norms that make communication possible. How prominent a role religion should take in this will obviously vary depending on the language being learned and how similar the associated culture is to the student's native culture. For languages such as Arabic, Pashto, and Urdu, religion is a relevant component. In the Middle East and South Asia religion shapes everyday life, and religious expressions are used in everyday contexts.

This exclusion of religion does not appear to be a universal policy at the DLI. Another respondent, who I will not name for confidentiality reasons, studied Russian at the DLI in the same time period. He reported that not only was religion included in the curriculum, but his class was required to attend a Russian Orthodox Church service.

Omar used class assignments and projects as an opportunity to bring Islam into the discussion, seeing its exclusion as problematic.

> I got to speak about Islam to my class and things like that and they were really into it 'cause hey we're learning about [an Islamic country], we should learn about Islam. It only makes sense. But that was only my class. They put how many classes through a year and I come here and I see the people who learned other languages that have to do with Islam, they don't know a single thing. And it's bad.

This void in the classroom seemed to allow common stereotypes and misconceptions to take hold among the students.

> And [the students] were like "Yeah, I heard that you're actually supposed to kill non-Muslims if you're Muslim." I can't believe how you got this far

learning the language and still think that. I mean all your teachers were from [Muslim countries], do you think they would teach you? [laughs] Are you alive right now? I mean they would've killed you if that was true. It's just common sense some of this stuff.

It is important to remember that Omar was talking here about advanced students learning specific languages to support the military mission. I was surprised that he reported these attitudes among these students, who I assumed to be more open-minded due to their education. However, throughout my interviews many of the specific examples of anti-Islam encounters involved those who should be most aware of these issues: linguists and those in intelligence. This may be because, as the contact hypothesis argues, while education can help break down stereotypes, it is not as powerful as actual contact. These individuals' studies focus on terrorism and extremist groups, which may make them more likely to engage in stereotyping than someone not engaged in this study who may have fewer opportunities to reinforce negative perceptions.

Omar also taught an optional class on Islam. Enticing students to attend with pizza, he used these classes as a venue to address common myths about Islam and Muslims.

Sometimes we had topics for the day but sometimes we just asked people to ask us questions. Because they're too nice to ask us about virgins and blowing yourself up and stuff, so we brought those subjects [up] and explained to them, hey this is not actually, this is just a rumor and things like that and then we'd give proofs and things like that. So they liked that, that we weren't just saying, "Hey, Islam's peace," we were actually giving proof. And a lot of people were coming because they liked what they were learning, but a lot were just coming for pizza [laughs].

Omar did not enjoy his military service, though he attributed much of this to a mismatch between his personality and military culture. He also experienced problems with leadership who saw his desire to work with an "Islamic language" as suspicious. Omar was able to effectively use EO protections to overcome this problem. However, in gaining access to this language training, he discovered a surprising reluctance to discuss anything related to Islam in the classroom. He found that this left space for troubling stereotypes to develop among the students. His presence allowed him to address these issues among his classmates, but he had concerns about the persistence of these negative ideas about Islam and Muslims among classes that do not have a Muslim student who is able and willing to speak up.

DANIEL: *ENTI MUSLIM?*

Daniel is a veteran who served for twenty years, much of it as a linguist. His experiences while deployed to the Gulf War led Daniel to convert to Islam. Daniel is white and was born in the United States.

Daniel told me that the opportunity for social and geographic mobility led him to choose military service:

> I was from a small town and my family was poor. [. . .] I'm a product of two non-college graduates, I'm from Small Town, USA where everybody doesn't go to college when I was growing up and they didn't know how to recommend what school or anything to you. They just, ok you graduated high school, time to get a job. I ended up going into the military, I thought it was cool.

Daniel did not go into the military anticipating that he would make it a career:

> I wanted to go in for two years, get some money and go to school, be the first one in my family to finish college.

However, responsive leadership worked with Daniel to find him opportunities that appealed to him, so he stayed for much longer. Eventually, the appeal of retirement benefits enticed him to remain for twenty years, although he felt that his opportunities had dried up.

> I was just like I'll stay in for a couple years and get out, but it kept going and going and then I had like eighteen years in. I was disappointed with the promotion and all that, I never really got promoted like I thought I should have. And there was eighteen years and I could have got out, but [. . .] I was like, hmm, let me think about this; I could either get out now at eighteen and just get a job and get nothing ever, or I could stay two more years and get paid every month for the rest of my life. Hmm, what should I do [laughs]. So I stayed in the rest of the way. But after twenty I just was done.

In general, Daniel was satisfied with the military lifestyle. As with many of the people who spoke with me, he felt that the military expanded his horizons.

How do I know that I would ever have taken *shahada* [converted to Islam] if it wasn't for the military. Living in Small Town, USA how do I know I would have ever had that exposure. How do I know that I would have ever met my wife, started my family, who knows.

As with Omar, Islam was something Daniel began to explore due to specific military experiences.

I was in Saudi Arabia for the [Persian Gulf] War and I'd see these people pull over on the side of the road to pray. I thought it was the coolest thing. [. . .] I learned so much, just kept learning more, and I became a Muslim.

As a white man with a typical American name, Daniel provides an interesting opportunity to explore how people are recognized or identified by others as Muslim. While most of the people I spoke with told me they were known as being Muslims due to their name or appearance, Daniel had neither marker. Perhaps because of this, when his commander was asked about the status of Muslims in the unit, the commander reported that there were none. This was despite the fact that Daniel played an active role in the Muslim military community.

The general called all the commanders and each installation had to report back to the secretary of defense: "Ok we're good here, all our people are taken care of." But then the people who were in charge of me reported, "Thumbs up, we don't have any Muslim soldiers," or something like that. And the general, I knew the general because I was the lay leader[1] on [base], he goes, "So [Daniel] doesn't work in your battalion anymore?" And [my commander] was like "Well yeah, he does but what about him?" "Well, he's just the head of all the Muslims on the base and downtown, but you don't know anything about him?" And they were so embarrassed.

Although he did not have any serious anti-Muslim encounters, Daniel did feel that Christian norms pervaded military culture, and this occasionally made him feel excluded.

That's probably my least favorite thing about the military, it's a Christian culture. I mean I was in it for long enough I understand it, but it's a very Christian culture. [. . .] If you don't believe in these values, you're not one of the good guys.

I asked him to elaborate on the Christian culture of the military:

> There's always a prayer before everything, let us pray, and praying for the country and the commanders, and the commander's kids, and his pets [laughs]. And then in Jesus's name, they always say in Jesus's name.[2]

Daniel also discussed the implicitly Christian nature of the annual winter "holiday" party:

> Everybody tries to be politically correct now, it's no longer a Christmas party, it's a holiday party, but every holiday party has a Santa Claus and a tree. And I'm like really, a holiday party? [. . .] I made the mistake a couple of times of calling it the Christmas party, and they were like "Oh no this is a holiday party." I was like, whose holiday is it? Whose holiday is in December? It's a Christmas party, we get it.

Daniel also independently corroborated Omar's observation that Islam was explicitly excluded from the language curriculum at the DLI. Daniel attended the DLI in the mid-1980s and again in the late 1990s. He said that even at that time, Islam was a touchy subject:

> There was a big Middle East contingent there, it was really very shy about staking a claim to Islam. [When I] went back for the refresher course [. . .] I'd see them on break and they'd whisper to me like *enti Muslim?* [Are you Muslim?] and I'd be like *tab'an* [Of course]. And they were looking around like they were so paranoid of somebody. And then I found out there were so many political things of hiring instructors.

According to Daniel's account of the DLI in the 1990s, the avoidance of discussion of Islam had little to do with contemporary tensions and more to do with sectarian divides within the faculty. He also described some of what he saw as the current issues:

> They went through a change [in] the 2000s because the Department of Defense was giving a lot of money for culture instruction.[3] [. . .] I asked them like where's your cultural stuff in here, when do you talk about this? They say that because they have native instructors in front of the class that's the culture piece. I'm like really?!? But yeah, I don't know how much they really talk about it, because it seems to me like it's inseparable.

Like Omar, Daniel recognized the important role of religion in gaining linguistic and cultural competence, particularly with Arabic.

I know so many people who graduated around the same time I did and they never talked about any religion stuff, although now I see everything is integrated because even non-Muslim Arabs say Allah,[4] they'll use *salaam aleikoum* as a greeting. We weren't taught that at DLI, we were taught *marhaba*.[5] And I'm like they don't even use it. [. . .] We didn't learn about Ramadan, I mean just the effect that month of fasting has on everyone in that area and anyone associated with the *deen* [religion]. At DLI you didn't learn about Ramadan, you didn't know Qur'an or *hijab*, simple stuff that everybody in the Middle East knows, whether Muslim or not. You didn't learn that at DLI 'cause they wanted to separate the culture or the religion from the language learning. Which I think is sorta ignorant.

The exclusion of topics such as Ramadan, *hijab*, and the Qur'an from an Arabic language class is a serious handicap for students who will be working in the Middle East. As Daniel observed, these are concepts that are highly relevant to everyday life in the region.

Like Omar, Daniel found that this void led to the use of inaccurate stereotypes about Islam, including the oft-repeated claim that Muslims are encouraged to kill non-Muslims. And like Omar, Daniel found that sometimes the stereotypes were so ridiculous that the only response was to laugh them off:

After 9/11, when people wanted to know about Islam and everything, it was like the most Christian person usually would try to give this [presentation] of what Muslims are supposed to believe and what they're supposed to do; about how the Muslims had to kill people in order to go to heaven. I was like really? I guess I need to know stuff like that, being a Muslim and all, thanks [sarcastic]. Sometimes I would [just] laugh.

Also similar to Omar, Daniel taught classes on Islam, working to address these misconceptions:

One of the classes I would teach was an Islam class. [. . .] We'd talk about jihad, probably one of the most misunderstood things about the *deen*, and I'd talk about the greater jihad, and the lesser jihad.[6] [. . .] At the end I'd say, for example, greater jihad can be teaching a bunch of military people about Islam, that's some Muslims' greater jihad. And they still didn't get it. And then I'd get these whispers "Are you Muslim?" I sure am. Why do people always whisper about it, it's like you have a disease or something. It's funny.

At the same time, Daniel was clear in his denunciation of the idea that only Muslims can or should teach about Islam:

My boss [would introduce me with] "Well he's a Muslim," and I went to him and said, "Hey, you don't have to tell people that, it's none of their business." Why would it matter if I'm able to teach the classes?

Omar and Daniel both identified situations where they felt excluded due to their being Muslim. Omar felt that the attitude of a specific leader negatively affected his career, though he did successfully utilize the equal opportunity system to address the issue. For Daniel, manifestations of this tension were much subtler, and like most of the people I spoke with, he didn't find that being Muslim significantly shaped his career. The cases of Omar and Daniel are also interesting for what they say about military education. Both worked as military linguists, and both studied at the DLI, though their sojourns there did not overlap. Between them, they provide a glimpse of military language learning over a period of more than twenty years. They independently provide reports of similar avoidance of any discussion of Islam in language training. The avoidance of this topic seems to allow a specific set of stereotypes to take root among language students.

PERVEZ: USING DIVERSITY FOR SUCCESS

Pervez is a veteran with a seven-year career in the military. A product of the ROTC system, Pervez served in the infantry and deployed to Afghanistan, where he was wounded. Pervez's parents emigrated from South Asia, and he was born in the United States.

Pervez explained how his father's experiences as an immigrant shaped his own sense of service:

My dad, he's always been a huge role model and a positive influence in my life, and he never really directly encouraged me to join the military, but he always talked about how America gave him all these opportunities that weren't available to him back home and he kinda talked about our lifestyle and our standard of living and how it was higher than, you know, what it would have been if you wouldn't have come to the States. And that just kinda formed a positive perspective I guess, of, you know, being in America and a great appreciation for everything that we had here. [. . .] While I was in high school I got this postcard for ROTC just like probably everyone going to high school gets as recruitment.

Pervez sent back the postcard and was contacted by a recruiter who encouraged him to check out the ROTC information desk during orientation at his college. This visit added practical reasons to join the military:

So I stopped by [the ROTC information desk], talked to them, and I found out more about the program [. . .] They told me "You can do it for the first two years and we'll pay for your tuition and you can walk away after two years if you decide not to serve." [. . .] So I said, "Ok, you're going to pay for my tuition, teach me first aid and how to shoot a gun? I'm in, sign me up!"

Military life agreed with Pervez. "I thoroughly enjoyed my time in the service, there's always up and downs but it was by far a positive experience in my life." In a familiar theme, Pervez contrasted the camaraderie of military life with civilian norms:

It's like you have a mission to accomplish and you focus on that and you come together as really brothers in arms. [. . .] It's just different when you're in civilian life and you have a project versus the military when you have a mission and it's just you and the men or women that you're working with and you are literally putting your life on the line for the mission and for each other and it forms this bond that is really incredible and you're literally shedding blood, sweat and tears for this mission and you're relying on each other, literally your lives are in the hands of each other and I think that's just an incredible feeling to have.

Pervez saw these aspects of military service as valuable life lessons:

You're focused on what you're assigned to do and I think that has a lot of merit to it. I think you gain a lot of maturity from those experiences. When you're so focused on a task and it teaches you. It's surprising how much it translates into civilian work or life, just your confidence without getting too cocky and also humility.

He also saw military service, and the travel and experience it provided him, as valuable:

> You gain when you see other parts of the world, you really gain an appreciation for what we have here. And you know, you find yourself not complaining as much; you're just satisfied with the little things in life and a lot of things that people take for granted. You can reflect back on the way people are living in some of the countries that you've worked in and you know I'd rather just be thankful for the world what we have rather than complaining for the little things, the comforts that we might be missing out on.

Pervez's parents were supportive of his decision to join the military, though after he was wounded they became more concerned.

> I was wounded in my first deployment to Afghanistan and that really affected my mother. I had a second deployment I had to go on and they were more concerned for my safety at that point than anything else because the reality kinda hit of the nature of my job.

After his initial tour of duty, Pervez's parents started expressing the desire that he continue his education, find a career, and start a family.

> When I told them that I wanted to extend my service they voiced some concern, not so much about my safety, but as any parents I guess they kinda wanted me to move on in my life. I was single at the time. They wanted me to further my education and come back. And they'd missed me 'cause I'd been far away from home. They kinda wanted me to come back to you know "settle down" and choose a long-term career path for myself.

In deciding to leave the military, Pervez considered family demands and the type of father he wanted to be.

> I stayed single the entire time I was in the military. I knew I wanted to get married and have kids. As much as *I* loved my life in the military, I personally, especially being a Muslim, I didn't really want to live married and family life while being active. And it's not like the military is a bad place for Muslim married couples 'cause I know Muslim married couples that were active duty and they had very strong marriages and stuff like that. But I watched the guys on my team, like on webcams, watching their kids open presents from them

on Christmas, and it's just like it's a huge sacrifice that they made, but I just, I kinda look back at the way my parents raised me and my dad was always there whenever I needed him, and I wanted that for my wife and for my kids, so I made the decision to leave the service.

Pervez was a practicing Muslim, and he was one of the few people I spoke with who reported being public in his religious practice: "I prayed in front of my guys, they knew exactly what I was doing." However, this wasn't his usual approach; he preferred to pray in private, not wanting to be seen as "showing off" and seeing religion as a personal matter.

For me it was like religion's always been more of a personal thing, so I wouldn't like go and deliberately pray in front of our men to show [off].

Pervez had no issues combining his religious and military roles, and he explained that while he was an ROTC cadet in college he was also a board member of the Muslim Student Association.

Pervez recognized that there was increased tension around his identity following 9/11, but he felt, as did many of the people who spoke with me, that it had little effect on him personally.

I know it's [discrimination] gone on, so I'm not going to deny that it does. But I never personally [experienced it]. I was always fairly confident in my faith.

Unlike most of the other people I spoke with who characterized at least some of the comments they heard about Muslims as being negative, Pervez perceived them as the results of curiosity, not malice. Also in contrast to most of the other people I spoke with, Pervez felt that members of the military in particular were able to see beyond stereotypes.

After September 11th, sometimes you'd hear comments, but it'd be more out of curiosity than anything else. And you'd be surprised the folks in the military now, where they've been, what they've seen, how much understanding they have of the Muslim faith and they can pretty easily distinguish between everyday Muslims and those that choose to use religion for bad reasons.

Pervez told me that his leadership clearly expressed the value they placed on diversity, and were happy to use his skills and background to their advantage, for example, after 9/11.

One of my unit commanders asked [me] to do a presentation on Islam, you know because a lot of people were very ignorant about what was going on, what was being said. So yeah, I've always been viewed as an asset in that regard and as an information source.

In addition, Pervez took on a leadership role in the field, reinforcing the value of diversity through his own leadership practices. As a practicing Muslim, Pervez found that his identity had benefits for the mission while he was deployed to Afghanistan. He felt that having a mosque on base was a useful tool for building rapport with local leaders and soldiers.

Whenever I got the chance I'd go, we actually had a small mosque that was built on our base, mainly for the Afghan soldiers and local village elders to use, but I'd go and pray with them.

Although he went to the base mosque to fulfill religious duties, not as a show to attract local attention, his presence created a chance to interact informally with Afghan soldiers and civilians, thereby building rapport while serving as a visible representation of the inclusiveness of the U.S. military. Pervez told me that the local civilian population he encountered was cut off from global communications and knew very little about the United States. In this context, Pervez saw his presence as having "a huge impact."

So when I walked in, being an Urdu speaker and also being Muslim, I mean one of the first things we do when we get on the ground is building what's called rapport with your locals and also your Afghan National Army soldiers, and it was instant for me. I mean they recognized my name, me being Muslim. I prayed with them and you know I met with the local villagers, introduced myself as Muslim . . . and especially when you're talking about a country where some of the villagers don't have any access to electricity, no TV, no Internet, so you can imagine what their perception of America is. So me coming in and introducing myself as an American, as a Muslim, can have a huge impact. Saying that I understand the religion, I understand the cultural dynamics. It was amazing how much respect the Afghan National Army soldiers gave me as well as the village leaders when I was there.

Pervez was well aware of the ways his identity as well as his cultural and linguistic competence helped him build rapport with local soldiers and civilians in Afghanistan. He understood this to be a benefit to the military:

No matter how much you get from the schoolhouse, nothing can replace me. At that point I'd had twenty-seven years being Muslim, being raised in a Muslim family, understanding things.[7]

The value of diversity was reinforced by the success of the unit. Pervez and his team were very good at what they did. According to Pervez,

We were very very successful with our mission in our area in Afghanistan. We created an environment that was very peaceful. We basically achieved mission success in our 5 to 10 km radius.

For the members of this unit, having a diverse team was something to be respected, something that contributed to their ability to complete the mission, and as an infantry unit in a war zone, success contributed to their personal safety. In a situation like this, the value of diversity was obvious.

Pervez also told me about the role his military service has played in his subsequent pursuit of a professional degree and employment.

My military experience is plastered all over my resume, so it's not like an official veteran hiring preference, but there's no doubt that I got the current position I'm in because of my military experience on my resume. [. . .] I think I'm a very unique individual being Muslim in the military post 9/11. There aren't too many of us like that. Yeah, it definitely helps.

Like most of the people who spoke with me, Pervez found being a veteran to be personally meaningful, but it was not something he liked to brag about:

I don't pound my chest with it or anything, no. If people ask about it, or are curious, I'm more than happy to talk about it. It's definitely something that I'm proud of as well, I'm not shy to talk about it. [. . .] But unless it comes up somehow in a conversation I don't force it, or introduce it into the conversation when it's not really a part of the conversation. Unless I'm getting a discount somewhere, then I'll drop it in a heartbeat [laughs].

Pervez felt that his background helped his unit achieve their mission. Part of this was due to language and culture skills, while another aspect was identity. Pervez's knowledge of a local language as well as his familiarity with the culture helped his unit effectively address issues in their region. In light of Omar and Daniel's discussion of the absence of this type of coverage in language training, Pervez's claim that "no matter how much you get from the schoolhouse, nothing can replace me" seems particularly relevant. In addition to his practical skills, Pervez also saw his identity, something that cannot be replicated through education and training, as an asset. While dealing with a population with little knowledge of global events, he felt he was able to stand as proof that the U.S. military is not engaged in an anti-Muslim or anti-Islam campaign.

JAMAL: STORYTELLER

Jamal is a veteran with a twenty-year career in the military. Of South Asian origin, Jamal immigrated to the United States as an adult. Jamal served in a specialized and senior position, and his service included time in a noncombat role in Afghanistan. For Jamal, positive experiences while immigrating shaped his desire to join the military:

> [The immigration official] said, "Well [education and IQ are] irrelevant, you're coming as a husband, you're married to an American." That was one of the most emotional moments of my life, I almost broke down. I could not believe that a rich country would be so governed by law, so governed by humanity, that they didn't care that I was a doctor or not a doctor, they didn't care if I was retarded or smart, just based on my value as a human being they were willing to let me immigrate. And at that moment I decided that this is a country worth dying for. And that's when I decided that I would eventually join [the military].

Jamal reported that he did not consider benefits, such as travel, as part of why he joined the military. He characterized himself as "a pure volunteer. [. . .] I was one of the very few people who joined out of generally patriotic reasons." He tells me that the recruiter he was working with was incredulous when he turned down various incentives. "I said 'No.' They said, 'Why are you joining?' I was kinda amazed, the only motivation could be a selfish one. And I said I'm joining just to serve my country."

However, he did note that an unanticipated benefit of his military service is the status it conveys on him as a brown man who might otherwise be treated with suspicion.

> What I did not anticipate of course was twenty years later as a brown-skinned Muslim man now [at] every airport I have to prove I'm not a terrorist and of course a military ID helps.

Jamal's parents took great pride in having a son in the military. He saw this as a generational effect. Jamal was one of the older people who spoke with me, having come to the United States as an adult with a family. His parents grew up in India while it was still under British influence. He explained:

What was important in their life growing up was the might of the British Empire, which was of course made evident through the might of the British military. So for them, my joining the military was a source of great pride. [. . .] During the British times the British recruitment policies favored big tall strong soldier races [. . .]. So the British army was mostly Sikhs or Punjabi Muslims. And people from my tribe, we were excluded from the Army, we were too small, too pathetic, too weak, too cowardly, or so the stereotype went. So when I could get into the military, from my parents' point of view that was a big success and they showed off about it incessantly.

Jamal contrasted his parents' reaction with that of his wife: "She was born after partition, she didn't grow up with the same mentality. [. . .] Her position was, what's in it for you? more of a utilitarian calculus of what are the benefits and what are the risks."

Jamal felt positively about much of his service. He described the opportunity to participate in missions that opposed terrorism as "uplifting." He also spoke about the sense of camaraderie that was so commonly mentioned in the stories people shared with me. His sense of this camaraderie was shaped by his age and position in the unit:

Now I look upon our soldiers like a father. I mean they were mostly in their twenties and I have a son who's in his twenties, so most of the soldiers reminded me of my son, and in a fatherly way, I really loved them. I have the greatest admiration for people who serve their country and these were people who had given up the safety of a very nice comfortable lifestyle back home and they were out there in the mountains of Afghanistan or wherever, and I felt very proud that I could do something to make their lives a little bit easier.

While his identity as a service member was a source of pride for his parents, Jamal anticipated that his Muslim identity would be a source of concern in the military, but he was surprised to find that it had little effect.

I don't think I was ever harmed by [being Muslim], in fact I was a little surprised it didn't come up. Somehow I thought that surely my Muslim heritage should have aroused suspicion a long time ago, but it apparently never did.

Jamal considered himself a Muslim by heritage only; he does not practice. The question of identity was one he struggled with when he was preparing for his first deployment to the Middle East. Asked what religion to list on his dog tags, he started by requesting that "Atheist" be listed since he had no desire for denominational care should he be injured or killed.

So I came home and I was about to be deployed in about a week and I'm showing off to my friends, a mixture of Muslims and non-Muslims, and I said, "Hey, these are my dog tags" and somebody said "Are you mad?! You've put atheist. You're going to Saudi Arabia, when they see your name and your religion as atheist they're gonna cut off your head. I mean if you're going to go to Saudi Arabia the best thing you can do is put Muslim on your dog tags because you're drawing attention to your atheism." So I said, "You're right." So I went back next day to the military [and] said I've had a change of religion, I'm now a pious Muslim, so they gave me new dog tags that said "Muslim," then I'm at another party with another group of friends showing off, and they said "Are you mad!? You're going to Iraq, when they capture soldiers, they'll forgive the Christians for invading Iraq, they'll forgive the Jews for invading Iraq, but when they see the Muslims invading Iraq they'll torture you. I mean a fellow Muslim, you'll be doubly tortured." So I said, "Oh gosh, you're right." So I went back to the military and said I'm not sure what to do. I can't put "Atheist" and I can't put "Muslim." [They] said, "Keep one of each, we don't care. Whatever you're wearing at time of death we'll bury you with that one." But that did invite me to think about what my religious identity is.

Jamal's work focused on terrorism. He felt that his South Asian Muslim background added depth to his work.

The strength of [my work] probably was that because of my Muslim heritage, I know of things that can't be proved by data, but I can understand certain nuances of language and looks that non-Muslims probably miss. So I've spoken to, I'm not saying that I've spoken to millions of terrorists, but I've spoken to millions of Muslims, and they have various degrees of political opinion. I'm probably more difficult to fool than someone else. I do speak

Urdu and I can pick up these very subtle nuances, especially in Urdu, which is a very poetic language.

Jamal also found that his background enabled him to build rapport with locals while he was deployed. While serving in Afghanistan, he encountered a man living locally. Based on their shared language (Urdu) they struck up an extended acquaintance. During the course of their chats they discussed Muslims in the United States:

> He said to me, "So what's it like in America?" and I said, "Life is wonderful," and he said, "How do people treat you?" and I said, "Very well." And he said, "They do?! They treat you well? But you're Muslim." And I said, "Can't you see? I [have a good career], I joined the military without any problems. [. . .] I'm a Muslim American, I live in a society where nobody messes with my religion, I can practice whatever religion I like, I joined the military, got promoted. It's a very fair society."

Jamal used his military service as an opportunity to demonstrate diversity and religious tolerance in the United States. In doing this, he served as a powerful counterargument to claims made by al-Qaeda and related groups that Americans are monolithic and anti-Islam. While I have discussed the contact hypothesis in terms of developing inclusion in the U.S. military, Jamal served a similar role for the local population and humanized Americans.

Jamal's interaction with this man continued, building on local traditions of storytelling. He recounted the following fantastical account:

> And he said, "Yeah yeah, [. . .] has anyone done anything *really* good for you?" [. . .] And then I remembered a story of a man I've never met. I said, "After 9/11 the Muslim community in America was fearful of a backlash. [. . .] The story that I heard was that [Dr. Fried] showed up for work and started growing a beard, and when he was asked why are you growing this beard, he said that "Most of my residency class are mostly foreign doctors and half the class is Muslim." He said "After 9/11 I want them to know, I want those with beards to know that I'm one of them. If anyone has a problem with my Muslim residents, they have a problem with me." It's a very powerful message for me. So I told this man that Dr. Fried, who I'd never met, did this apparently. And the man in front of me was large, mean-looking, tough-looking, it wouldn't have surprised me if he had one foot in al-Qaeda. I would not want to be alone

with him in some Afghani cave or anything [laughs]. He was spellbound at my story and his eyes became teary. [. . .] So he says to me, "This man must be rewarded." I said, "I'm sure God will give him his reward." He said, "No no, I have to reward him." [. . .] So I said to him, "You're not without influence, you can commit an act of charity I'm sure." I said, "I'm pretty sure that Dr. Fried is Jewish, and I'm pretty sure that most Jews fear that if they're caught by al-Qaeda they'll be very harshly treated. So if you have this influence and you want to reward Dr. Fried why don't you give me permission to inform Dr. Fried that in his name any Jewish prisoner that you capture will not be treated harshly, and that will be his reward." And he said, "That's very difficult for me to do, that's a war decision, I don't make those decisions and that may not go down very well with my people." And I said, "Well do you think it went down well with Dr. Fried's people? After 9/11 it showed enormous courage, enormous character, and if you don't [have the character] he doesn't want your carpet and trinkets and whatever." [. . .] He said, "Okay, tell Dr. Fried he has six lives." So I have no idea who that man was. I have no idea if this was a game he was playing with me, I have no idea if he was sincere or insincere, and there's no way I can check or anybody can check. [. . .] But you know there is a tradition of storytelling in Afghanistan, so I'm pretty sure that this man told the story of me to many of his friends, and I'm sure he said that "I met a Muslim and gosh, guess what, he lives in America." It's not impossible that he tells this story as well. I'm hoping that generates a certain environment of compassion, mercy, love.

Through a shared language and a shared appreciation for the art of storytelling, Jamal introduced this man to a complex vision of America where Muslims and non-Muslims can form friendships and where, in the wake of 9/11, some Americans stood with their Muslim friends and neighbors rather than against them. A facility with the cultural norms of storytelling, and also an understanding of cultural norms of honor and respect, helped Jamal humanize American service members, and he hoped that this would have a long-term positive effect.

SIX

BEING MUSLIM AND AMERICAN

Many of the people who spoke with me articulated a sense of patriotism and national belonging that shaped their decision to join the military. They saw themselves unequivocally as Americans. In some of the stories they shared with me, the importance of being both Muslim and American stood out particularly clearly. Sometimes these moments were elicited by expressions of the assumption that one must be either Muslim or American. Through dialogue and education, these service members and veterans challenged these assumptions and claimed a space as both Muslim and American.

In this chapter, I present four narratives that specifically illustrate this theme. Ahmed reveled in breaking stereotypes, both those of other people and his own, and found that military service presented many opportunities to broaden his horizons and those of people around him. Yusuf, a combat soldier, engaged in everyday education and was valued by his unit for this, and his service was used by his parents to educate the public. Rahma was very clear in making the connection between valuing the United States and choosing to serve in the military. She also engaged in active dialogue and education and saw herself as a bridge builder. Hakim saw it as a responsibility to engage in dialogue and took his decision to educate those around him very seriously. He built bridges both with other service members and with locals in Afghanistan and Iraq.

AHMED: BREAKING STEREOTYPES

Of the people I spoke with, Ahmed had the longest career in the military. He had served for over twenty years, and was still on active duty when we spoke and had no immediate plans to retire. As an aviator, he had served all over the world, including in Operation Enduring Freedom in Afghanistan. Ahmed is an immigrant from South Asia.

He identified as a moderately practicing Muslim. He fasted and organized Friday congregational prayers on base, but also said, "I'm not really religious." Ahmed told me he did not seek any formal accommodation for fasting, preferring instead to work it around his regular duty schedule.

> I've actually fasted and I've broken my fast in the airplane. [. . .] Nobody ever told me I couldn't, it was a very personal decision, and if I knew I could do it then I did it. And my colleagues knew that I'm fasting and you know, they would make fun of me, "Yeah we saw him eating a date in the airplane" or whatever because the sun had gone down.

Ahmed told me about organizing congregational prayers in the military:

> On every base that I've been stationed on I've always set up the Friday prayer. And so every Friday whether I attended or not we had the opportunity to pray our Friday prayer. [. . .] Before 9/11 I would get a couple of dozen Muslims [. . .] but then after 9/11 I would run into Muslims and I'd say, "Hey listen, we do Friday prayers, would you be interested?" And quite a few of them would say, "No, I'd rather not tell somebody I'm Muslim."

Ahmed's observation supports the supposition that official tallies of Muslims in the military undercount the actual population because, among other reasons, many Muslims may choose not to reveal their religious affiliation. It is apparent from this statement, and those made by other people, that a number of Muslims in the military seek to downplay their religious identity or "pass" as non-Muslim. Due to the structure of this project, I did not talk with anyone who was in this situation, and so the experiences or expectations that led these individuals to hide their Muslim identity cannot be addressed here.

Ahmed enjoyed his military service and found the military lifestyle rewarding; his experiences had even encouraged his daughter to pursue a military career.

> I've had a fantastic time, I enjoy [my work], and I've moved up the ranks. It's all been good, and honestly people ask me, "How long you going to stay?" And I tell them I've not even thought about getting out because it truly has been an absolutely phenomenal experience. And you know the stuff that we

do is absolutely amazing. Yeah, there was no question I was going to stay in, and I have a daughter who wants to be an officer. It has just been a very positive experience for the whole family. And I mean it's not an easy life, it is definitely very tough. [. . .] In the military, life is not for everybody, but if it's for you I think it's a fantastic career.

Ahmed grew up wanting to fly. He came to the United States to study as a young man and was influenced by American popular culture, leading him to choose the military.

Since as far back as I can remember, I always wanted to fly and I was interested in military aviation. [. . .] I was seventeen when I started flying, then eventually I came to the United States. After I finished up college I was going to go back to fly for the national airline there. But then I saw *Top Gun*, and I thought you know what, this sounds way better than flying for an airline.

Initially Ahmed's father was disappointed in his decision to stay in the United States and join the military rather than return to his birth country.

[My father] basically was hoping that I was going to go back and pick up where he was going to leave off. And so he was very disappointed, he didn't speak to me for two years and then he came to visit me and then everything was okay.

For Ahmed, one of the best parts of military life was the opportunity to broaden his horizons and meet new types of people.

After I joined the military I met people from all parts of the country, which was absolutely phenomenal, and because I met people from all parts of the country I met an ex–Ku Klux Klan member, and then I met people who were extremely liberal, extremely accepting, maybe not very religious. So basically I met the gamut. For me that was an absolutely fantastic experience.

Ahmed spoke at length about how positive it was for him to meet people from such different backgrounds and walks of life. His experiences with diversity in the military had a profound impact on him and on how he thinks about himself.

That is really when I started feeling like I was an American, and I felt that if they accepted me and I accepted them, and even though they felt like there's something different about this guy, we got close enough to where they could joke about my religion or about my background. So I was one of the boys, but I was a little bit different, and that was okay.

Although he did not use the jargon of social science, Ahmed clearly explained the idea of the "contact hypothesis" as he elaborated on how the military context created a space where prejudice could be successfully broken down.

> That is one thing that's so beautiful about the military, that you take folks from every corner of the United States, every different background, you throw them together and sure enough, because of this assimilation most of the people come out a little bit better. So that's kind of been my experience, and during this time I met some extremely racist people and I met some people that I knew thought of me as some evil terrorist or something, and that's another thing in the military because we are an equal opportunity organization. You can't openly go out there and make accusations or make fun of somebody because the repercussions are pretty severe.

While the military brings together diverse populations, it also provides structure and constraint on these meetings. Whatever their personal feelings, service members must comply with behavioral norms of inclusion, and if they fail to do so, there is a clear way to address and correct this behavior; this context sets the stage for breaking down prejudice. As Ahmed put it:

> The military helped me break some of [my stereotypes], and conversely I was able to help break some of the stereotypes that Americans had of Muslims.

Ahmed also discussed how this diversity played out when dealing with the militaries of other countries, particularly when meeting with Muslims from other countries.

> When I would deploy outside the United States, I would come in contact with Muslim officers from different nations and they would ask me "Listen, how are you treated?" And so to help break some of those barriers was pretty positive. I came to this country with a lot of stereotypes, and those are the same stereotypes that a whole bunch of Muslims, when they come to this country, they have those stereotypes and not until you actually get to know the people that you have some of these feelings about, you know you can't break those barriers until you're actually given a chance, giving yourself an opportunity to meet and get to know, and then when you do, you realize, hey we're all the same.

Ahmed did occasionally encounter anti-Muslim ideas among his colleagues, but these were never targeted at him.

> I've had this happen, where, you're part of a group where somebody will generalize, and they'll call all Arabs terrorists, or, they'll say oh yeah camel jockey or whatever, they'll call names, or they'll just make just a very generic statement. So that happened where somebody would just say something negative about Muslims and then go, "Oh my gosh, we have a Muslim," and then all turn and look at me.

He also related a specific story of encountering this attitude among two intelligence officers. Disgusted, he confronted them:

> There are a couple of intelligence officers that were making fun of Muslims. And so I sit there and I listen, and they had no clue that I was a Muslim, and so then I told them "You know what, you guys are ignorant." I said, "If you've got a question you can ask me 'cause I'm a Muslim, but don't just go out there and spread stuff that's not accurate 'cause you're supposed to be intelligence officers, and you're officers and you shouldn't conduct yourself that way."

As we discussed his experiences as a Muslim in the military, Ahmed told me he had been concerned that being Muslim would negatively affect his career, but he was surprised to find that this did not seem to happen. A few years after 9/11 he came up for a prestigious promotion:

> So I thought that with my name and the fact that I was a Muslim, and this is post-9/11, I thought there was no chance I was gonna get selected. But I was. And when I [got the position] I became the very first Muslim [in this position], and that is after 9/11. That for me was very positive 'cause I thought you know what, we are equal opportunity, this war is not on Islam, and in the military we reward people that work hard.

Ahmed also shared a moving story that belies the simplistic view that the United States is at war with Islam or Muslims as a general category. While deployed, the unit Ahmed was with found the body of a local civilian who appeared to have died in an accident. Ahmed was called to help the chaplain perform Muslim funerary rites in order to bury this man with honor and dignity.

> One day I got a phone call: "Hey listen, the chaplain wants to talk to you." So I went to see the chaplain he said, "Hey listen, we found a dead body and we're

not sure where he's from, but we have a feeling he's [from the region]." And so the U.S. authorities contacted the [relevant] nations and said, "Hey listen, this might be your citizen, would you like to claim him?" And the countries said, "No we don't." The chaplain had contacted me so that I could do the Muslim prayer that you do before you bury somebody. [. . .] It really moved me because I thought here it is, I myself am flying missions in support of this operation and there are people that are saying it's a war on Islam. But we found a dead body and just because we think this guy's a Muslim we want to bury him with dignity. And so I did the ceremony.

Throughout our discussions, Ahmed provided clear examples of how institutional characteristics of the military can positively shape the experiences of diverse service members. Ahmed meets service members from a variety of backgrounds, and in turn sees his own background as a contribution to a general project of breaking down barriers and stereotypes. For Ahmed, the military provided a safe space for this with formal policies in place to address any problems.

YUSUF: RELIGION IN COMBAT

Yusuf served in the infantry and was on the front lines. Raised in South Asia, Yusuf immigrated to the United States as a teenager and joined the military out of high school. Yusuf decided to join the military for a variety of reasons:

It was a collection of factors. I wasn't sure what I wanted to do. I was always fascinated by the military. And I thought as a Muslim I had something to contribute back.

Yusuf also mentioned the role of the media in his decision to join the military:

I was like show me some videos, I was really motivated. I saw *Full Metal Jacket* [laughs]. That was it.

When I asked him about being Muslim in the military, Yusuf told me that he felt that the context of the current conflicts made his Muslim identity visible.

You were certainly aware that you're Muslim, especially 'cause of the conflicts. But if the conflicts weren't happening it would not be an issue at all.

Yusuf felt that his colleagues identified him as Muslim from his name; however, he felt that it didn't change how he was treated.

As soon as they saw my name tag [they knew I was Muslim], but it was just like being part of any unit, I never had a problem. [. . .] I think it's no matter who you are, as long as you perform, that's how you're gonna be known. You sleep with them, train with them, do almost everything with them. You become sort of a family. You don't feel like you're different.

This is another example of the power of strong leadership and unit cohesion. Yusuf identified the unit as "sort of a family," and because he was contributing his fair share, he was fully included. The context of being in a combat unit may also shape the importance of actions in building trust. In the war zone, Yusuf's unit had a clear shared goal—stay alive. In the face of this overwhelming shared goal, differences in race, national origin, and religion lost importance. The group became highly cohesive not because members were similar to each other, but because they were working toward the same goals, and the more successful they were, the greater trust they had in each other.

Yusuf experienced times when his identity as a Muslim was verbally used against him, but similar to Mahmood, he perceived this to be a part of hazing traditions and saw it as equivalent to the treatment received by his colleagues, and therefore as a sign of inclusion.

One time in boot camp I did get hazed and the drill instructor was like "Are you part of al-Qaeda or something" and he was going off on me. But he'd go off on other people, you know, "You look funny." So I don't think he specifically did that to me, but I remember that happening like once or twice when I was getting hazed, doing push-ups and they were shouting in my face. They try to break you down so they might have thought let's break him down this way.

As a member of the infantry, Yusuf deployed multiple times and served on the front lines. His primary characterizations of combat were confusion and senselessness:

We would go into the city, different houses, just lost. At times getting frustrated, throwing things around, getting angry at the Iraqis. 'Cause there's [different] personalities within your unit, so you know some have a breaking point, a threshold for confusion, less than others. It was a different, I mean, I guess I'm trying to get at it's a, it was a very weird experience in its own right. I would not, if I had the option, go through it again.

Yusuf saw the chaos and destruction of combat at firsthand:

> Things happen for no reason, like your buddy gets blown up, dies in front of you. Like what the hell. One minute he's laughing, next minute he steps on an IED and he's dead.

When ordered to deploy again, Yusuf was reluctant, but expressed a commitment to the ideas of service and duty:

> I was reluctant to go back, but as a soldier I knew that I had a duty and I wanted to complete my duty to the best of my abilities. I didn't agree with it but it's politics and it's not the first war or the last war. I just try to keep my hands clean. You know, don't shoot until you're shot at, no innocents, so I had my own moral ethics I tried to follow. And I think for the most part I did it and I'm proud of that.

Yusuf told me that he drew heavily on his faith to cope with the stress of combat:

> I would pray a lot. But not physical like five-time prayer. In my heart. Just say some of the common prayers, the small prayers in the Qur'an that I knew by heart, and God would always be on my mind going on missions, you know, don't let this man be killed on my hands, protect me and my unit too. Things like that.

Religious practice has long been recognized as a part of war and a response to stress. The military historian John Keegan argued that religious observance is a vital part of preparation for battle.[1] The historian Alex Watson in his examination of combat resilience among British and German troops in World War I found that faith on the battlefield tends to have more to do with a sense of spiritual connection with divinity than with formalized religious traditions.[2] Yusuf articulates this in distinguishing his battlefield religious practice from the formal ritual of *salah* (five daily prayers). In their study of American soldiers in World War II, Stouffer et al. found that prayer was a common strategy for coping with combat.[3]

The role of religion in the reintegration and healing process of veterans has recently begun to be discussed as well. The religious scholar David Bosworth argued that "religious traditions appear to be a valuable but underutilized resource in the treatment of veterans."[4] He argued that existing research on post-traumatic stress disorder (PTSD) focuses on things done to or witnessed by the soldier, but disregards the psychological stress of killing and the effects of feelings of guilt over actions in combat. Bosworth uses the biblical term "bloodguilt" to describe this sense of post-combat guilt. Martin Cook, a professor of leadership at the U.S. Naval War College, sees PTSD as an issue for psychology and psychiatry but also as a spiritual concern. He suggests the usefulness of considering the implications of military service spiritually and bringing "moral ambivalence, guilt, and post-traumatic stress explicitly into the spiritual conversation."[5]

Yusuf expressed some of this sense of ambivalence, and he saw his faith as relevant to his conduct during combat and as an important component in processing his experiences.

> When I look back, sometimes there's a conflict as a Muslim, did I do some-thing wrong, 'cause I went and participated in this operation. But then I say if God truly is unbiased, and we're judged on our intentions rather than what happened,[6] I see that my intention was not to hurt any innocents regardless of who they were. As far as I know I accomplished that, so I can be at peace with myself.

After leaving the military Yusuf immediately returned to school, and he credited the structure and support provided by his family and by his confidence in the morality of his own conduct with easing his reentry into civilian life.

> Civilian life, it wasn't as hard 'cause I came back to my parents, they supported me, I had a structure. But since I've gotten out, in the company five people have killed themselves. For me it wasn't so bad when I think of them. I did struggle to make sense of what I want to do in life and sometimes it would just hit me what I had gone through. At that time when you're going through it you just think of staying alive, getting through the day, looking out for your back and for your buddy's back. But when you're back you think of, it seems like a movie, where you've been. I mean those things will probably never happen to me again. The things I did, the things that happened.

His return from the war and his reentry into the civilian world felt like a new start.

> I went right away to school, 'cause like I said I was very motivated, 'cause I thought I had a new life, a sort of new beginning. After we came back from deployment, the first thing when you touch ground you're like we made it! You know, fully intact we made it. [. . .] I took some preparatory classes 'cause my math skills had gone down. But I found that I had another set of skills, like

I could concentrate better, on studies I could motivate myself, the discipline which I didn't have before in school. Also I had that drive to do well and make something out of myself. I didn't take things for granted.

Despite the trials of combat, Yusuf found his military service to be an extremely rewarding experience. When I asked him what the best thing about serving in the military was he responded immediately:

Discipline. They give you self-confidence. Friends that you made while you were in the service. Just camaraderie in general, even when you get out.

Yusuf felt like a full member of the unit and did not feel singled out because he was Muslim. At the same time, he found that his background was useful to his unit in explaining cultural and religious issues that they encountered. Yusuf felt that his experience and advice were particularly valuable for his comrades because of the inadequacy of pre-deployment cultural training.

[Pre-deployment cultural training] was poor, I'd give it a poor rating. The guys would just warn you don't do this, don't do that, and that was what cultural training was. I mean simple things, like don't wave with your left hand, say *salaam aleikoum* to everyone. They would say it to everyone. What they don't get is it's good to say that, but after a little while they're just gonna think you're annoying. There's no point in the little Arabic you know to keep throwing it out. You know someone just comes and says, "Howdy, howdy" to an American you'd be like, "What, is he an idiot?" That's what a lot of these Iraqis looked at us like. Who are these idiots? What are these idiots doing here?

On the ground, Yusuf served as an informal resource when members of his unit had questions:

They would ask why is it bad to show the sole of the feet? Why is it bad to use your left hand? Why is it bad to say certain things or to handle the Qur'an? Why is it bad to come with your shoes on inside the house? Why are they so nice to us, the Iraqi people, even when we're searching their houses, turning the house upside down, there's shooting outside, why do they still offer us food? So I explained to them that it was the Arab culture, and more broadly the Islamic culture. Just give them some details so they have better understanding.

Yusuf's family also benefited from his military service by using it as a way to defuse tense situations in the civilian world. Yusuf's parents occasionally encountered people who made hurtful comments about Muslims. They used Yusuf's military service to negotiate these conversations:

> [My parents] both have customers coming in and they talk. So like the average American would say like "These damn Muslims are like ruining the world" or just "What's wrong with them?" So they would say, "Oh I'm a Muslim and my son is serving in the military," and then they'd say, "Oh we didn't mean it in that way, say thank you to your son."

Of the people I spoke with, Yusuf shared the most detailed accounts of life in combat. For Yusuf, as for generations of soldiers before him, religion was an important mechanism for coping with the stress and uncertainty of combat. Being Muslim American intimately shaped his experiences in combat and the way he coped with the memories of these experiences. Back at home and enrolled in a civilian school, he reflected on his experiences through a lens of ethics based on his faith and used his certainty that he did not break his own moral code to help process his experiences. Yusuf also found that his familiarity with the local language and culture was valued by his unit. Having been subjected to poor pre-deployment cultural training, his colleagues often sought him out to explain the practices and customs of the local population. Thus, he helped his unit achieve their mission in a way that no one else could.

RAHMA: BUILDING BRIDGES

I met Rahma about a year before I began this project. When I began speaking with people for this project I contacted her, and she agreed to participate. She is a veteran with a six-year career in the military, where she worked in a support position. She decided to leave the military to be closer to her family and to start a family of her own. Rahma is white and was born in the United States. She converted to Islam while in the military.

Family tradition played a large role in her decision to join the military. "For me it was kinda carrying on tradition." A sense of service and loyalty to the United States was also a component of her decision. Although Rahma was native-born, she grew up abroad and much of her family lived in Europe, so living in the United States was an active choice.

> It was serving my country that I chose to be in, 'cause I could go but I chose to be here. I chose to live in the United States 'cause I think this is a better place to live.

Rahma's family was generally happy with her decision to join the military, perhaps because of the family tradition. However, she felt that her gender made her decision particularly confusing for other Muslims:

> The community that I frequented, they were the whole "Oh my gosh, but sister[7] how are you in the military!?" They were all shocked about it, about the family aspect of it. They weren't shocked about me being a Muslim, they were more shocked how would you reconcile your family with your military work, you're gone for months on end.

Many Muslims subscribe to an idea of complementary gender roles. In this view, husbands are financial providers for the family and wives have primary responsibility for children and the household. However, this does not mean that women are expected not to work. The Pew Research Center found that 90 percent of American Muslims agreed that women should be able to work outside the house.[8] Here the issue was not that Rahma had a job, but the time commitment of serving in the military, and especially the possibility that a deployment would take her away from her family.

Rahma also discussed how being a service member transgressed expected roles of femininity within the civilian Muslim community she was a part of:

> If you [say] you're in the military the guys won't even give you a second chance. So it was sort of like a dating disaster and I wanted to settle down so I made a more conscious decision to settle in one place without the possibility of them shipping me out to the desert months after I've had my baby.

Rahma enjoyed her experiences in the military. As with most of the people who spoke with me, she saw her service as broadening her horizons.

> Just the opportunity to go to any place at any time. That was a great positive experience, and just the, when you join the military, if you put your mind to it you have so many open possibilities, [. . .] the possibilities and the opportunities that the military itself presents you are limitless if you put your mind to it. So just to have that I think that is one of the greatest positives you can get out of the military.

It was through these types of opportunities in the military that Rahma came to Islam.

My first deployment [was] to [a Middle Eastern country] and that's actually what started my search for Islam was because I wanted to figure out a bit more about who we were going to be interacting with, what do they believe, how do they live and everything. So shortly after that I converted.

She also valued the sense of community she felt in the military:

There's so many [positive experiences]. Being deployed and meeting so many new people, you build such camaraderie with them. It's friendship and it's like brotherhood and sisterhood between all these different people, and in some instances you become closer than family. That was one of the greatest positive experiences that I've had in the military.

After leaving the military, Rahma found that she missed the fellowship and competence of working with her military colleagues.

You miss the military camaraderie, the whole brotherhood and sisterhood that you get for people, you miss it. There were the deployments where you go out someplace and it is just you and a group of people and that's it, you guys have each other's back and you know nothing will happen to you because these people are competent in their jobs.

As a white convert who did not wear *hijab*—the headscarf—in uniform, Rahma was not immediately identifiable as a Muslim. Her identity, however, was a matter of public knowledge, and she informed her commander and colleagues following her conversion. She did not think that her identity as a Muslim had any effect on her military career:

I never really had any major issues. I had some stupid comments here and there, you know, "The Muslims, the Muslims," but it wasn't really anything directed completely towards me, it was more like a general statement that was being made in my hearing, but I never took it personally.

She took an individualistic perspective on her success, and argued that her achievements were the product of her personal effort and not affected by her identity. She also recognized the role of leadership:

I think if there would have been a disadvantage or anything that I missed out on it would've been more something that I didn't achieve personally rather than something that was affected because I was Muslim. Again I was lucky with my team command because they really [cared about] my achievements personally rather than what my belief system was.

Rahma's leadership was accepting of her conversion, and open to providing accommodations as needed. The command structure demonstrated an investment in diversity by reaching out to her to make sure her needs were being met.

As the only Muslim in the unit, I was approached a few times by the chaplain, or even the command, asking me, "Hey look, are there certain special requirements that we need to give you guys for certain holidays? Is there anything special that we need to do when we go overseas? We all have our briefings when we go, but we want to hear it from you just to make sure it is the right information."

Rahma regularly sought formal accommodation for religious practice and did not have any issues getting it. During Ramadan she sought accommodations to alter physical training (PT) requirements:

We met at dawn to do PT, so not having any fluids or anything, it got hard. So I went to the commander at the time and I said look these are my requirements during this month and I would very much like to observe this. Do you have any issues with it, or do you have any suggestions on how to get around the PT requirement? [. . .] So he [sent] me to the PT NCO and we came up with this plan that on the days that we're supposed to do PT in the mornings I would be there but I would be there as like a water person, you know, handing out water, I would assist with getting the times for their runs and everything, and make sure people are hydrated and all that, but I myself would do PT at night. [. . .] That's how we worked around that.

By not excusing her from dawn PT, this accommodation normalized religious diversity in the unit. She was not absent from early morning trainings, which could become a source of resentment, and her altered presence (handing out water and writing down run times) made the accommodation visible, making it clear to the whole unit that diversity could be effectively accommodated.

As we talked about her family, Rahma reflected on the protective nature of the military and American society generally. Her sister, who is also Muslim and who lived in Europe, had many negative interactions.

She's been physically attacked, prodded by old people with umbrellas just sitting at the bus station and yelling at her, "Go back to your own country" and she's like "I'm born and raised here, I am in my country." Her kids have been attacked. She's gotten discriminated against. So all the experiences that she's experienced, I'm glad to have not had that here, that's one of the reasons I choose to be here. That's one of the reasons why I'm glad in the military. I really never got a whole lot of that; there'd be one or two incidences where somebody would mention something but that was not directed towards me.

Rahma was proud of her military service:

I'm proud to be a veteran and I'm proud to be Muslim. And I'm actually going to be sworn into the VFW [Veterans of Foreign Wars] Post as an official member, and I'm going to be the first Muslim veteran at this VFW Post. [. . .] It's not something I would have made note of 'cause it's just part of who I am, but they made a note of it and that's how they announced it.

While she was proud of her service, she felt that it is "not something to brag about; [it] is just part of the service that you did for your country." Rahma also directly connected her military services and her sense of citizenship:

I've had the whole people staring at me when I walk down the street if I have a scarf on my head or "Oh yeah, go back to your own country." I can constantly just ignore it 'cause I know I am in my own country, I've served for my country, and they most likely didn't; though I don't know their background just as much as they don't know my background.

Rahma also talked about her role as a bridge builder. She negotiated and educated others in the military about her faith, she had confidence in being Muslim American in the public sphere because of her service, and she worked to carve out a space as a veteran in the civilian Muslim community. She talked about this role with confidence and a sense of responsibility:

I can be a liaison. Like in the mosque people talk about the military in Iraq or Afghanistan, I feel confident in my voice, "Hey look I was in the military and that's not really how it is, it's more like this." And the same as when I was still in the military, [. . .] when they talk about "Oh, the Muslims this, the Muslims that," I can be like "Well hey, that's a myth, that's something that you see on TV that's [perpetuated] by the media, not actually something that goes on in our everyday lives, that's not something that we do." You know we don't go around screaming *Allahu akhbar* with swords in our hands and burning the American flag. So I feel more confident in my voice talking to either one of the communities and dispelling myths or saying hey look this is the real deal, this is how it really is.

Being able to serve as a bridge and a source of information was an experience that Rahma greatly valued.

I think that's one of the greatest things about being Muslim in the military, that you get the chance to get so many questions where you can answer, where you can set the record straight. We're not all terrorists, no, we're not all crazy fanatics strapping bombs underneath our burkas [laughs]. Some of us are pretty good people, in fact [the] majority of us are pretty good people.

Rahma had positive experiences in the military, due at least in part to supportive leadership. She recognized the powerfully unique position she was in as a Muslim veteran and used this identity to speak out in both civilian and military spaces.

HAKIM: STANDING UP FOR HIS RIGHTS

At the time we spoke, Hakim was currently serving and had put in eighteen years. He did not have plans to retire anytime soon. Hakim had worked in various support specialties, and when we spoke he was in the process of furthering his education in preparation for his next post. Hakim had deployed to both Afghanistan and Iraq. An intellectually curious youth, Hakim had been studying Islam before joining the military, and he converted soon after. Hakim is multiracial and was born in the United States to immigrant parents.

For Hakim, the decision to join the military largely stemmed from the military service of his family.

Well, I'm a military child. My father [. . .] enlisted before I was even born. [. . .] So when it came time for me to decide what I wanted to do, for me it was I wanted to join the military. That's what I grew up with.

For Hakim, the military was a familiar environment, and he derived comfort from the discipline of it. When he attended a civilian college he felt lost and decided to leave school and return to the military, this time as a service member.

All my life up until that point I had only dealt with military children and military schools, so going to a civilian public university was just complete culture shock. It was like "What in the world? These people are wild! They don't have discipline and order in their lives." I just couldn't deal with that, so the military was the environment I needed to be in. [The military] allowed me to remain focused on my goals and objectives in life.

Hakim discussed the opportunities presented by the military and the way it had broadened his horizon:

I can't even imagine at this point doing something else. The United States military is a diverse organization. It's a microcosm of the reality of America. [. . .] It's an eye opener. [. . .] The experience has allowed me to go through life without the blinders, that tunnel vision. I've been able to see a bigger picture, the horizon's a lot wider, and I would say God's grace is a lot bigger than the limitations that people put on it. So I'm good with it, I enjoy it.

Hakim told me he had experienced some tension around his identity, though he noted that it was not limited to the post-9/11 world. As a new convert in the 1990s, he felt that even at that time some people saw Muslims as "other."

I'd just become a Muslim and [. . .] there were individuals that didn't take very well to the idea because of their misinformation, their ignorance, etc. [. . .] and so people had their preconceived notions, their stereotypes, their generalizations.

Hakim wore a kufi,[9] a skullcap worn by some Muslim men, and so was easily visually identifiable as Muslim.

Ever since I joined the military I've always worn a kufi or a *taqiyah*, the religious headgear, because there's authorization for it. In civilian clothing I wear it, but in uniform I wear it as well. I see that it's allowed so I'm going to do it. [. . .] It's not a statement, it's just what I do as an expression of my faith, very similar to those that wear a cross around their neck, or when Jews [wear] the yarmulke, it's no different. It's an expression of faith.

Since 9/11, he had experienced some tensions around his identity such as general comments, name calling, and occasional suspicion.

After 9/11 I do recall people making comments, you know you get the e-mails and things of that nature. But one guy he made a statement to me, I forget what exactly he asked me, but it was as though there was this assumption that all Muslims know one another. Like I have Osama bin Laden on my speed dial, and can say, "Hey, you need to quit this nonsense." It was really ridiculous.

Like most of the people I spoke with, the incidents Hakim encountered were minor, and his reaction was to laugh them off and to engage in a dialogue. Hakim took a very active role in claiming a space as an American Muslim service member by addressing tensions and stereotypes when they arose.

When I hear a comment being made I'm quick to address it. I'm pretty vocal. And I think I'm that way 'cause that's the only way people are gonna become educated. You have to address the ignorance; you can't just let it slide, like oh, they just don't know any better so I'm just not going to say anything.

Hakim also engaged in formal education, providing, for example, presentations on Islam during which he directly addressed some stereotypes.

I've had wonderful, I can see them as learning experiences, learning opportunities when someone challenges me in a presentation: "Well you know, doesn't the Koran say to kill the infidel?" I mean just remarkable. You can tell they're just repeating what they've heard on the news or something they may have heard in a conversation with someone else; it's just repeated propaganda. So the presentations I give I actually put that on a slide, those few words: "Kill the unbelievers wherever you find them," and then on the very next slide I show the entire context of the verses[10] and I say, "Just read that." And they're sitting there reading, and they're like "Wow." And I'm like "Do you have a different impression now that you see the context of that verse?" And they're like "Yeah it doesn't say that at all." It's like yes. So next time, just open the book up and read it for yourself and don't be spoon-fed.

Hakim took a very active role in defending his rights. He saw this as a responsibility and emphasized the importance of Muslims speaking up for themselves in order to define their experiences rather than be defined by others. He feels it is important to stand up for his rights and the rights of other Muslims in the military.

I'm outspoken, I definitely let my voice be heard. And I deal with whatever consequences may [be]. I know the Constitution, and I know the military regulations, and I know what I can say and what I cannot say. [. . .] I would say that there is a responsibility for Muslims in the military to study up and find out what their rights are, to know what they can and cannot do.

Hakim also addressed the role of informed and strong leadership in implementing religious accommodation. While Hakim himself was well-versed in regulations regarding religious accommodation and was not shy about standing up for his rights, he observed that his right to wear a kufi in uniform had been repeatedly questioned by those unfamiliar with these policies.

People have had an issue with the religious headgear, and every single instance I've found out it's because they have not read the regulation. Every single time. And it's on page two. It's very clear, it says very clearly, it describes the religious headgear; it says that it's authorized. It says what the color has to be, the size of it. It gives all those descriptions and yet I've come across a number of senior-ranking officers and senior enlisted that are like "Are you authorized to wear that?" I'm like, wow, have you not read the regulation, that's one of the most common regulations in the military, how could you not read that? [. . .] Seriously, it's just a matter of education.

Taking the time to read and understand the regulations regarding religious accommodation demonstrates an investment in diversity. It is, as Hakim observed, a matter of education, but it's also a matter of caring. Leaders who do not bother to familiarize themselves with these types of policies communicate that it is not worth knowing the rights of minority service members.

Hakim, like several other people who spoke with me, felt that being Muslim gave him particular insight.

It's one thing to learn about Islam academically and not experientially. [. . .] You may understand this [theology], but in the practical aspect, in the social aspect, in interacting with people and different interpretations and different responses, that takes on a whole other study in and of itself.

Hakim used this cultural competence in his military tasks interacting with locals in Afghanistan and Iraq.

What has ended up happening both in Afghanistan and Iraq is [my commanders] see how I interact with locals and how they respond to me and it's like someone observes that and is like "Hey, you know what, can we use you in a different capacity by talking to the locals, establishing rapport, interacting with local businesses, businessmen and other personnel?" And so I'm like "Yes, of course."

This experience of interacting and building rapport with locals was a common one among the people I spoke with who deployed to Afghanistan or Iraq.

More than just being able to easily interact with locals, Hakim found that he was able to serve as a representative of the inclusiveness of American society.

Interacting with the locals, I came to find out [they] didn't even know 9/11 happened. And that was so insightful. We were like wow, these people don't have a clue, they're just as ignorant as you can assume, obviously the literacy rate is quite low, but the fact that they didn't have access to radio, television, etc. They just saw us as an invading force. They were not aware of why we were there. [. . .] So for them to come across me, they were like "What?! You're a Muslim?" [. . .] But it was good 'cause they have been told up to that point that the foreign devils—Americans—are coming here and just like the Russians and British before them. They're against Islam; they're against Muslims and so on and so forth. So I'm sitting there explaining to these local Afghans and tribal leaders that no, that's not the case. I told them Islam is flourishing in the United States, we have mosques and Islamic institutions and charities and we're free to practice our faith. I'm explaining all of this and they're just looking at me in amazement, like are you serious?! Like this can't be possible [laughs]. I'm like I have photos, I can show you. This is real.

Having leadership that valued the skills and knowledge Hakim brought shaped his experiences for the better.

I've taken every opportunity to try to engage in dialogue with people and fortunately I've been under the command of individuals who take advantage of that. They see that we have someone born and raised as an American, military child, is a Muslim as well, has been deployed, is involved with the local Muslim community, and I've been utilized to build bridges of mutual respect and understanding. And it's been fantastic.

Rather than treat him with suspicion, Hakim's leadership actively used his differentness to help them achieve their missions.

SEVEN

THE DIVERSITY OF THE MUSLIM
MILITARY EXPERIENCE

The preceding chapters explored some of the diverse experiences of Muslims serving in the U.S. military. Since 9/11, the dominant narrative in American society has been one that treats the identities of Muslim and American as being mutually exclusive. The events of 9/11 and the subsequent invasions of Afghanistan and Iraq reinvigorated very old stereotypes that defined Muslims as dangerous and fundamentally incompatible with American life. Policies targeted Muslims and anti-Muslim sentiment grew, as did violent expressions of this hatred and fear. Within this time period, thousands of Muslims chose to serve in the U.S. military. Using in-depth interviews with fifteen Muslim service members, this book considered the varied experiences of this group that clearly defies the idea that one must be American *or* Muslim. The stories shared by Muslim service members and veterans challenge this dominant narrative and encourage much more nuanced reflection on what it means to be Muslim American.

DISCUSSION OF THEMES

Many of the people who spoke with me had positive experiences that reflected their own personality, their fit with the military lifestyle, and their willingness to pursue the opportunities presented by military service. As with any population, these experiences were varied. Just as it would be foolish to speak about "the Lutheran military experience," it is similarly useless to speak of a monolithic shared experience for Muslim service members. Some loved the discipline, for example, Hakim, who left civilian school to join the military, while others, such as Omar, hated it.

Although there were many differences in the military experiences of the people who spoke with me, there were also some recurring themes that should be noted. Many of the stories I've related here included descriptions of a sense of service:

I feel like the country's given me so much and I am doing my share to pay back (Mahmood).

I wanted to do *my* part to serve the country (Zafir).

[My father gave me] a positive perspective of being in America and a great appreciation for everything that we had here (Pervez).

It was serving my country that I chose to be in (Rahma).

This sense of service was often connected to experiences with immigration. While popular stereotypes often portray immigrants in general and Muslim immigrants in particular as less "American" than native-born citizens, the service members and veterans I spoke with often saw being immigrants or the children of immigrants as what made them want to serve in the U.S. military. This was a recurring theme in the stories I heard that powerfully challenges stereotypes about Muslim Americans.

Another recurring theme was the sense of camaraderie described in many of the stories I've related here. This was the most consistent answer when I asked about the positive aspects of military service. The other most common answer was the opportunities presented by military service to expand their horizons, a confirmation that the contact hypothesis remains useful in understanding military service. Both of these themes speak to the inclusion of these service members and veterans. To see camaraderie and meeting new people as defining positive aspects of service demonstrates that for most of the people who spoke with me, they were included in their units. These themes demonstrate that they felt a part of the camaraderie and were comfortable enough in their inclusion to seek to broaden their horizons. Again, these themes challenge stereotypes about Muslim Americans; given the opportunity, these service members and veterans became part of the unit, base, and branch they served in. They may have been different in some ways, but they were also accepted for the many ways they were the same. As Ahmed put it, "So I was one of the boys, but I was a little bit different, and that was okay." That this process of integration generally worked is a positive reflection on the American ideal of *E pluribus unum*, "out of many, one."

The Muslim service members and veterans who spoke with me were obviously aware of the challenges facing them as Muslim Americans at this moment in history. While most of the people who spoke with me did not think that being Muslim negatively affected their time in the military, many did share stories that conveyed the sense that they were set apart in some way. For example, many of the people who spoke with me related hearing jokes or stereotyped comments about Muslims. Mahmood and Yusuf both told me of being targeted with epithets such as "al-Qaeda" during basic training. While common, these examples tended to be minor, and the people speaking with me did not seem overly concerned by them. For the most part, the people I spoke with felt like full members of their units. They worked toward shared goals with their colleagues and felt that their abilities were respected by others. Many were surprised that their being Muslim was not treated as a problem. This may be a product of the military setting.

Mahmood enjoyed the opportunities presented by his military service, especially the chance to meet diverse people. Despite some concerns that his identity would negatively impact his career, he felt that he was never treated differently because he was Muslim. Kareem also felt that the military offered him many opportunities, and he saw the emphasis on equal opportunity as an important factor in making sure the diversity in the military remained beneficial rather than a source of conflict. Kareem also noted changes in the atmosphere after 9/11. While he sees increased stereotypes about Muslims in both the civilian and the military worlds after 9/11, he also sees an increased awareness about diversity within the military.

MILITARY STRUCTURE

The military has certain characteristics that can facilitate the integration of diverse groups, such as the hierarchy of the organization and formal equal opportunity policies and procedures. For several of the people who spoke with me, formalized EO procedures made the military a protective environment in the face of negative attitudes about Muslims. For example, Basim noted the difference between the military, where hate speech can be directly addressed, versus the civilian world, where there is little accountability for such behavior. Several people utilized military equal opportunity offices to address instances when they felt their Muslim identity was affecting their military careers, and most were successful in addressing the immediate problem; for example, Omar used the EO office to get a new assignment, and Zafir used the EO office to deal with harassment from a commander.

However, not everyone found the military structure to be helpful. For Sadia, the military structure that required the accusations made by her ex-husband to be taken at face value led to a disruptive investigation. The presence of EO policies could not help her as she faced an intensive investigation, gossip, and unsupportive leadership. For Farid, the needs of the military that demanded his deployment to Afghanistan put his family in Pakistan in very real danger. Again, EO policies could not mitigate these effects because the issue was not one of discrimination but one of military need versus personal vulnerabilities.

LEADERSHIP

Leadership emerged from these stories as an important factor. Leadership is a central component of U.S. military culture and plays a crucial role in the success or failure of efforts to integrate diversity in the force. Sadia described this succinctly: "It really depends on where you get sent and who is in charge and who your supervisor is and all sorts of stuff like that." Leadership that saw value in diversity and was invested in supporting it created a positive atmosphere. However, leadership that repeated stereotypes or fears created toxic environments in which Muslim service members felt excluded.

I shared two cases of strong leadership and two cases of weak leadership. For Tarek, a leader set an example of support. Following a troubling encounter, his colleagues rallied around him, allowing him to contextualize the experience as minor and exceptional. Najib experienced the benefits of institutionalized religious accommodation during Ramadan at a service academy. The normalization of this accommodation made Najib feel included and like a valued member of the team. Later in his career, Najib served with a leader who modeled the value of cultural competence. Although Najib did not serve in a unit with a language, culture, or intelligence mission, his commander valued cultural competence and even held himself up to this standard by learning Arabic and engaging in dialogue with locals to improve his cultural understanding. In this way he was not just paying lip service to the importance of diversity, but was demonstrating the value he saw in diversity through his own actions. Najib saw good leadership as a defining piece of his story:

It's a good feeling when your boss trusts you to do something; to go out on your own and do it. [. . .] That's when I felt a little bit of pride. Right now I would say I'm really just proud to be a military guy; I'm happy with the work that I'm doing and my boss now tells me that he appreciates my work every day.

On the other hand, Zafir spent a short career consistently at odds with a commander who he reported called him names, accused him of supporting the enemy, and singled him out for poor treatment. Basim felt that his previously positive experiences soured following 9/11. Questioned by security and denied religious accommodation, Basim felt insulted and degraded. In these cases, the people who spoke with me left the military earlier than planned and with negative impressions. Both Zafir and Sadia reported that other minority service members were negatively treated in their units (Zafir alleged racism against black service members, while Sadia described the harassment of Latter-Day Saint [Mormon] service members), which suggests that the poor leadership may create a generally toxic environment.

DIVERSITY AND MILITARY MISSION

Diversity is increasingly recognized as an important element for military effectiveness. The important role of diversity came up in various ways during my conversations with service members and veterans. Omar and Daniel bemoaned the lack of effective cultural training in language classes. Pervez and Jamal demonstrated what a powerful tool cultural competency can be.

Omar and Daniel, who did not know each other, both made very similar observations about the absence of Islam in language training at the Defense Language Institute. Both saw this as a problem, and this void seemed to create space for negative stereotypes and misconceptions among students. The absence of nuanced discussion of issues such as the use of religious texts by insurgents allowed students to grow more convinced in their own stereotypes. In addition to creating an unwelcome atmosphere for Muslim American service members, this was problematic because a nuanced understanding of how religion and culture is used by extremists to achieve political ends is crucial to military success. Stereotypes that claim violence can be explained simply as "us-versus-them" will not make the world a safer place.

Interestingly, though with only fifteen respondents it is merely suggestive, is the tendency of the people I spoke with to identify those making stereotypical comments as affiliated with language and intelligence positions. For example, in sharing a story of officers making fun of Muslims, Ahmed explicitly identified them as "a couple of intelligence officers" and saw this as particularly problematic. "You're supposed to be intelligence officers, and you're officers and you shouldn't conduct yourself that way." Tarek prefaced his story about the woman who was "a little racist" toward him by describing the base he was working on as being near a large intelligence community. Both Omar and Daniel reported advanced language students sincerely believing that Muslims were required to kill non-Muslims. Omar, Zafir, Basim, and Sadia, who all had negative experiences that they attributed to being Muslim, all worked in language or cultural specialties. The negative stories I heard were concentrated in language and cultural specialties stateside, while the people I spoke with who saw combat had some of the most positive things to say about their experiences. Perhaps this is due to seeing the practical value of diversity in the combat zone. For a unit which sees that having diverse colleagues makes their mission easier, diversity will be treated positively. Likely this difference is also a product of the different nature of in-group and out-group thinking under combat conditions. In the combat zone, the in-group is very viscerally (and clearly) defined as those not trying to kill you. The importance of trusting unit members under these conditions will override other possible schisms. On the other hand, most of the negative cases stateside were in office-like settings. This perhaps encouraged office politics and gossip.

BEING MUSLIM AMERICAN

Given the context of post-9/11 society, I expected that many Muslim service members would engage in negotiating their identity as Muslim Americans as a reaction to popular assumptions that they must choose whether they were Muslim or American. Many of the people I spoke with recognized, either explicitly or implicitly, the tensions of the current context, and they engaged in varied strategies to carve out a space where they could be seen as complete human beings with multiple (but not necessarily competing) identities.

Ahmed enjoyed the opportunity to meet other service members from various backgrounds, and clearly articulated the important role the military hierarchy played in making these interactions positive. Ahmed also saw himself as an important element of military diversity, and he used his position in the military to help break down stereotypes about the U.S. military in the Muslim world.

Yusuf was seen as an asset by others in his unit because of his cultural competence. As part of a combat team, he did not have to engage in much discussion; his actions and the usefulness of his knowledge demonstrated that he is both American and Muslim. As he puts it, "I think it's no matter who you are as long as you perform." His parents used his military service to challenge the assumptions of people who had accepted stereotypes of Muslims as not belonging in the United States.

Rahma engaged in bridge-building activities. A source of information for her unit, she also took on the role of dispelling stereotypes about both Muslims and service members. She saw her combined identity as giving her a unique perspective which she was eager to share. Hakim engaged more directly in negotiation. Like Rahma, he saw it as a responsibility, and a privilege, to engage in dialogue and education, explaining and demonstrating the compatibility of these identities. Hakim was quick to stand up for his rights and literally engaged in a display of uniformed difference as he wore religious headgear in uniform. In the face of us/them pressures he redefined a world in which being Muslim American is not just a possibility, but a reality. Hakim and Pervez both used their identity as Muslim Americans to build rapport with locals in Iraq and Afghanistan.

MILITARY SERVICE AND CITIZENSHIP

While working on this project, I often found myself drawing comparisons with the experiences of Japanese Americans during World War II. Nisei, second-generation Japanese Americans, successfully used military service in World War II to renegotiate their position in society from suspected enemy to model minority. With the onset of World War II Japanese Americans were stigmatized for belonging to the same ethnicity as the enemy, and on the West Coast, Japanese residents (including U.S. citizens) were interned at desert camps.

Initially banned from military service, Nisei were given the opportunity to serve in special all-Nisei units. These units were intentionally designed as a way by which Japanese Americans could demonstrate their loyalty. The all-Nisei units served admirably in the war, receiving many military awards and favorable media coverage.

Despite some parallels in the treatment of Nisei and Muslims as "others" based on acts of war and terrorism carried out by people who looked like them, the stories that I heard were quite different from those of the Nisei. While the

Nisei often explicitly framed their military experiences in terms of citizenship, this frame was largely absent in the stories I heard. This is not to say that the stories I heard did not include patriotic themes, but the people who spoke with me did not tell me that they were serving as a way to prove themselves as Americans. Rather, they were serving because they already saw themselves as Americans. This variation may come down to differences in official policies targeting these groups.

In the civilian context, the negative treatment of the Nisei was much more formalized (and more extreme) than the treatment of Muslims following 9/11. Although there were early fears that something similar to the evacuation and internment of the Japanese would happen to Muslims, it did not. There are some parallels, for example the policy from 2001 until 2011 requiring the registration of young men from certain countries. However, the registration policy did not force relocation of individuals, nor did it target the entire Muslim community, focusing instead on a specific subpopulation of noncitizens. Disruptive as it was to many families, the policy did not include the wholesale rounding up and relocation of the Muslim community. In addition, the official rhetoric of the "War on Terror" sought to distinguish the enemy (terrorist) from Muslims. Although this did not fully work, this is a very different context than World War II when Japanese and Japanese Americans were explicitly and officially associated with the enemy, and even U.S. citizens of Japanese descent were treated as "enemy aliens."

Japanese Americans were also subjected to official discrimination in the military, being declared ineligible to serve in 1942. When they were allowed to serve the following year, it was primarily in segregated, all-Nisei units. On the other hand, Muslims have never been formally prohibited from joining the military, nor has their service been segregated.

The absence of formal policies of exclusion makes the case of Muslims since 9/11 quite distinct from that of Japanese Americans in World War II, so it is no surprise that these groups would have different stories. Japanese Americans employed a narrative of citizenship, and they used their military service to claim citizenship for themselves, their parents, and their children. This does not form a salient part of the stories I heard, probably because the citizenship of Muslim Americans was not threatened in the same way. At the time I spoke with these people, there had been no formal calls to strip Muslims of their citizenship and no policies that officially treated citizens as noncitizens because of their Muslim identity. The people I spoke with told me about choosing to serve not because they wanted to become Americans, but because they already felt American.

It is also important to question the connection that is drawn in American society between military service and sacrifice and citizenship. A critique of the militarization of citizenship is far beyond the goals of this project, which is to explore the untold stories of a particular population. These stories need to be told and so do the many other stories of untold service, which can take many forms. The connection between military service and citizenship has a long history in the United States, but it is certainly not the only way in which minority groups "prove" their value to American society.

WHAT WE CAN LEARN FROM MUSLIM AMERICANS IN THE MILITARY

The stories presented in this book add to the growing body of literature that challenges the claim that being Muslim *and* American is impossible or even difficult. Among the Muslim service members and veterans who spoke with me, not one expressed a sense of tension between being Muslim and being American. For example, Pervez was at ease being an ROTC cadet and a leader of the Muslim Student Association, Rahma joined the local chapter of the VFW, and several people brought up popular culture, from *Full Metal Jacket* to Tom Clancy to *Harry Potter*. When confronted with assumptions based on their Muslim identity, they engaged in dialogue and negotiation. These people embodied what it means to be both Muslim and American.

WHO IS SEEN AS BEING MUSLIM

As I discussed in chapter 1, Muslims are difficult to accurately identify based on external characteristics such as skin color or appearance. Though the stereotypes about this group in the United States often assume that Muslims share a "brown" phenotype, this is factually inaccurate; there are Muslims of many races and varied appearances. Individuals of certain national descent, such as South Asians and Arabs, are commonly, and often inaccurately, believed to be Muslim. At the same time, Muslims are often treated as if they are a cohesive ethnicity.

This is useful in thinking through a few examples from the people I spoke with. As a white man with a typical American name, Daniel (chapter 5) provided an interesting opportunity to explore how people are recognized or identified by others as Muslim. While many of the people who spoke with me discussed being identified as Muslim due to their name or appearance, Daniel had neither external marker. Perhaps because of this, when his commander was asked about the status of Muslims in his unit, the officer reported that the unit did not have any Muslims, despite the active role Daniel played in the Muslim military community.

Dress is also a characteristic used in the United States to label someone as Muslim. Only one of the people I spoke with, Hakim (chapter 6), wore religiously identifiable attire while in uniform, and he did note that this elicited responses from people about his identity. Rahma, one of the women I spoke with, wore a *hijab* (a headscarf) but only when she was not in uniform. Her decision spoke to the role of external labeling:

> I never wore *hijab* while I was in uniform but [my commander] did say if I wanted to I could fill out the forms and everything and they would support me in that decision. I just never took that step 'cause I felt that if there was some type of comments being made, even if it wasn't directed towards me, I didn't want to aggravate or instigate or whatnot.

Rahma recognized that wearing a *hijab* in uniform would mark her as different, and perhaps subject her to comments that had previously not been directed at her. Since Rahma did wear a *hijab* when she was dressed as a civilian, she experienced the way this piece of fabric could shape interactions.

> I've had the whole people staring at me when I walk down the street if I have a scarf on my head or "Oh yeah, go back to your own country."

Name is another marker of Muslim-ness that may shape the experiences of Muslims inside and outside the military. I asked service members and veterans how their colleagues knew they were Muslim, and name was the most common response:

> [The patient] looked at my name badge, she was friendly, she wasn't angry towards me at all, and she's like "Oh are you Muslim?" So I said, "Yeah I am" (Tarek).
> I mean they recognized my name, me being Muslim (Pervez).
> As soon as they saw my name tag [they knew I was Muslim] (Yusuf).

This tendency is not limited to identifying Muslims; social scientists have long been aware of the way in which names are used to make decisions about how to view and interact with a person. In American society, names are generally believed to convey information about gender, race, ethnicity, and religion. In turn these identities are believed to convey something meaningful about the character and habits of the person him- or herself. In a study on housing in Los Angeles County, the researchers found that applicants with Arab-sounding names were less likely to get a positive response than applicants with white-sounding names (though more likely to get a positive response than applicants with black-sounding names).[1] A similar study in Toronto found that applicants with Arabic or Muslim names were the most likely to be discriminated against.[2] The anthropologist Shahram Khosravi sees the use of names to communicate stereotypes as a legacy of larger processes; drawing parallels with anti-Semitism, he argues, "Muslims are turned into *a* Muhammad. Like the Cohen regularly featured in anti-Semitic jokes and songs, the name Muhammad also often figures into jokes about Muslims."[3]

The role of appearance, attire, and name in identifying these people as Muslim should serve to remind us of how pervasive stereotypes are about Muslims. These stories should also point out the shortfalls of these stereotypes. Kareem spoke of people using skin color to identify Muslims but without any understanding of cultural (and religious) differences, treating Bangladeshis and Moroccans as interchangeable. Rahma introduced the complex calculus many Muslim women go through in deciding how to get dressed every morning. Several people remind us that the legacy of negative views about Muslims and Islam have made it seem reasonable to distill complex global identities into the few syllables on a name tag.

The Muslim American community presents a complex case for understanding external labeling. Being "brown" is often associated in popular culture with being Muslim, but this measure is often inaccurate. Attire and name are also used as ways to identify Muslims. Some members of this community may find themselves identified by a combination of all of these characteristics, while other members can "pass" on all of these markers. In addition, being Muslim is a fluid identity. Some individuals will rarely if ever be assumed by others to have this identity, while others may find themselves given this label even if they don't identify with it. For example, Jamal explained:

> I'm actually an atheist, but culturally I'm a Muslim, I have a Muslim name, so in a sense I've got the worst of both worlds. At the airports, [there are] hassles because I'm Muslim, and I go to a Muslim restaurant for a good meal and of course everyone hates me 'cause I'm an atheist.

IMPORTANCE OF INSTITUTIONAL DIVERSITY

Leadership that is supportive of diversity may arise out of abstract ideological commitments, but in this project it also seemed to commonly occur in units where the practical value of diversity was clear. For example, the people I spoke with who served in Afghanistan and Iraq often noted that their language and/or culture skills were valued by team members who saw the practical value of working with other service members who could communicate effectively with locals. In cases such as these, diversity was a clear advantage for the unit, and so there was a practical reason to value and support inclusion.

Many scholars have noted the ways in which the natures of the conflicts in Iraq and Afghanistan have differed from wars such as World War II. Whether it is characterized as "unconventional," "asymmetrical," or "fourth generation," the nature of these conflicts shapes the need for quality training and investment in developing culturally competent troops. Cultural training and cultural competency have become components in successful mission accomplishment. Beyond classroom training, personal contact with diverse colleagues is crucial to developing cross-cultural competency.

Many of the people I spoke with felt they contributed to military missions through their language and culture skills. Languages spoken by my respondents included Arabic, Urdu, and other Middle Eastern and South Asian languages. While language and culture can be learned by anyone, several respondents also discussed the subtleties of language, dress, and behavior that they were attuned to through growing up in Muslim communities. The people I spoke with served as both formal and informal teachers.

CONCLUDING THOUGHTS

When I started this project I expected to hear similar stories from Muslim service members and veterans. I expected being Muslim to have fundamentally shaped their experiences in the military, and I expected them to speak about their experiences in ways that paralleled those of Japanese Americans who served during World War II. Many of these expectations and assumptions were complicated when I actually began speaking with Muslim service members and veterans. What stands out from the stories I have related here is that the experiences of Muslim service members and veterans are shaped by a myriad of factors.

Certainly my formal education in military sociology helped me to see common threads related to military structure, leadership, cohesion, and other concepts academics like to write about. However, the experiences of the people who spoke with me were shaped by many factors beyond the measurable variables I set out to explore. They were shaped by personality and attitude: Omar the pacifist, Sadia who wakes up one day and decides to join the military, Hakim who longs for the structure and discipline of the military lifestyle. They were shaped by family: Mahmood's wife who patiently deals with missing furniture, Rahma's future children who prompt her to seek a more settled lifestyle, Ahmed whose daughter now wants to pursue a military career herself, Pervez's mother who is shocked when he is wounded and is reluctant to see him deploy again. They were shaped by personal faith: Yusuf who found comfort in knowing that his moral intentions were pure, Daniel who is moved by witnessing civilians in Saudi Arabia praying, Kareem who as a teenager fasted long days in 120-degree heat, Najib who didn't fast for years. They were shaped by global political forces that prompt particular immigration patterns, by vagaries of the economy that shaped employment opportunities, by the everyday particularities of their lives: being in the right place and time to perform funeral prayers for a deceased civilian, waiting in line at a butcher shop at the same time as someone who despises you, breaking the fast in an airplane, working the night shift when a child got sick, stopping by an ROTC table at college. Whether we think of it as fate, God's will, or random chance, it's the combination of these and many other factors that shaped the array of stories I was entrusted with. At the end of the day the stories I related here could be the stories of any Americans. The people who spoke with me told me stories full of hope and joy and stories of tragedy, and many stories that fell between these extremes. Being Muslim is just one part of the experiences I have described here. While it is important to ask how Muslims are faring under current social and cultural conditions, it is also important to remember that Muslims, like any minority group, are complex, diverse individuals. There is no "Muslim experience" of life in the United States or even of military service during a specific time period. Rather, there are experiences of individuals that to varying degrees are shaped by, among other things, being Muslim.

NOTES

INTRODUCTION

1. FBI, "Hate Crime Statistics," 1996–2014, http://www.fbi.gov/about-us/investigate/civilrights/hate_crimes.

2. David Crary, "AP Series about NYPD Surveillance Wins Pulitzer," Associated Press, April 16, 2012, http://www.ap.org/Content/AP-In-The-News/2012/AP-series-about-NYPD-surveillance-wins-Pulitzer.

3. Lori A. Peek, "Reactions and Response: Muslim Students' Experiences on New York City Campuses Post 9/11," *Journal of Muslim Minority Affairs* 23, no. 2 (2003): 275.

4. Ibid., 280.

5. Samuel P. Huntington, "The Clash of Civilizations?" *Foreign Affairs* 72, no. 3 (1993): 22–49.

6. Ibid., 73.

7. Ronald R. Krebs, *Fighting for Rights: Military Service and the Politics of Citizenship* (Ithaca, NY: Cornell University Press, 2006), 17.

8. James Burk, "Citizenship Status and Military Service: The Quest for Inclusion by Minorities and Conscientious Objectors," *Armed Forces and Society* 21, no. 4 (1995): 503–29; Krebs, *Fighting for Rights*, 183.

9. At the time only whites and individuals of African descent were eligible for naturalization.

10. Lucy E. Slayer, "Baptism by Fire: Race, Military Service, and U.S. Citizenship Policy, 1918–1935," *Journal of American History* 91, no. 3 (2004): 848–49.

11. Tamostsu Shibutani, *The Derelicts of Company K: A Sociological Study of Demoralization* (Berkeley: University of California Press, 1978), 39.

12. Mike Masaoka with Bill Hosokawa, *They Call Me Moses Masaoka: An American Saga* (New York: William Morrow, 1987); Shibutani, *The Derelicts of Company K*, 98.

13. Jess Staufenberg, "Khizr Khan's DNC 2016 Speech: Read the Full Transcript from the Grieving Muslim Father Who Addressed Donald Trump," *Independent,* July 29, 2016, http://www.independent.co.uk/news/world/americas/dnc-2016-khizr-khan-donald-trump-read-full-transcript-father-muslim-soldier-a7161616.html.

14. Ghazala Khan, "Trump Criticized My Silence. He Knows Nothing about True Sacrifice," *Washington Post,* July 31, 2016, https://www.washingtonpost.com/opinions/ghazala-khan-donald-trump-criticized-my-silence-he-knows-nothing-about-true-sacrifice/2016/07/31/c46e52ec-571c-11e6-831d-0324760ca856_story.html.

15. Alexander Burns, Maggie Haberman, and Ashley Parker, "Donald Trump's Confrontation with Muslim Soldier's Parents Emerges as Unexpected Flash Point," *New York Times,* July 31, 2016, http://www.nytimes.com/2016/08/01/us/politics/khizr-khan-ghazala-donald-trump-muslim-soldier.html.

16. Even those who are opposed to the military recognize the large role the military plays in U.S. society. See, for example, Cynthia Enloe, *Does Khaki Become You?* (London: Pluto, 1983).

17. Pew Research Center, "Muslim Americans: No Signs of Growth in Alienation or Support for Extremism," 2011, http://www.people-press.org/2011/08/30/ muslim-americans-no-signs-of-growth-in-alienation-or-support-for-extremism/.

18. During Ramadan, practicing Muslims abstain from food, drink, and sexual behavior from about an hour before dawn until sunset. The fast lasts for a lunar month, about twenty-eight days.

19. Andrea Elliott, "Sorting Out Life as Muslims and Marines," *New York Times,* August 7, 2006, http://www.nytimes.com/2006/08/07/nyregion/07marines.html.

CHAPTER 1

1. Denise A. Spellberg, *Thomas Jefferson's Qur'an: Islam and the Founders* (New York: Alfred A. Knopf, 2013), 280.

2. Norman Daniel, *Islam and the West: The Making of an Image* (Oxford: One World, 1960); Karim H. Karim, *Islamic Peril: Media and Global Violence* (Montreal, Can.: Black Rose Books, 2000); Edward Said, *Covering Islam: How the Media and the Experts Determine How We See the Rest of the World* (New York: Vintage Books, 1981).

3. Daniel, *Islam and the West,* 17.

4. Karim, *Islamic Peril,* 2.

5. Spellberg, *Thomas Jefferson's Qur'an,* 15–17.

6. Ibid., 188–96.

7. Ilyas Ba-Yunus and Kassim Kane, "Muslim Americans: A Demographic Report," in *Muslims' Place in the American Public Square,* ed. Zahid H. Bukhari, Sulayman S. Nyang, Mumtaz Ahmad, and John L. Esposito (Lanham, MD: Alta Mira, 2004), 311.

8. Spellberg, *Thomas Jefferson's Qur'an,* 121.

9. Michael A. Gomez, *Black Crescent: The Experience and Legacy of African Muslims in the Americas* (New York: Cambridge University Press, 2005), 161.

10. Ibid., 143–84.

11. Spellberg, *Thomas Jefferson's Qur'an,* 273.

12. Geneive Abdo, *Mecca and Main Street: Muslim Life in American after 9/11* (New York: Oxford University Press, 2006), 71.

13. Martha M. Boltz, "Davis' Camels a 'Hi Jolly' Glory," *Washington Times,* October 18, 2003, http://www.washingtontimes.com/news/2003/oct/17/20031017-080128-5646r/.

14. Abdo, *Mecca and Main Street,* 61–86.

15. Spellberg, *Thomas Jefferson's Qur'an,* 277.

16. Abdo, *Mecca and Main Street,* 61–86.

17. Ibid., 63–64.

18. Ibid., 82.

19. Estimate of 3.3 million provided by Pew Research Center, "A New Estimate of the U.S. Muslim Population," January 6, 2016, http://www.pewresearch.org/fact-tank/2016/01/06/a-new-estimate-of-the-u-s-muslim-population/. Ba-Yunus and Kane, "Muslim Americans," provides an estimate of 5.7 million Muslims in the United States.

20. Selcuk R. Sirin and Michelle Fine, *Muslim American Youth: Understanding Hyphenated Identities through Multiple Methods* (New York: New York University Press, 2008), 44.

21. Although Indonesia has the largest Muslim population of any country in the world, Indonesians make up a very small proportion of the Muslim population in the United States. Ba-Yunus and Kane, "Muslim Americans," estimate that Indonesians make up less than 3 percent of the Muslim population in the United States.

22. Karim, *Islamic Peril.*

23. Peter Gottschalk and Gabriel Greenberg, *Islamophobia: Making Muslims the Enemy* (Lanham, MD: Rowman & Littlefield, 2008), 61–88.

24. Huntington, "The Clash of Civilizations?" 27.

25. Ibid., 35.

26. Daniel Pipes, *Militant Islam Reaches America* (New York: W.W. Norton, 2002), 125.

27. Ibid., 140.

28. In Islamic jurisprudence, *taqiyyah* is the practice of dissimulating about religious beliefs under conditions of extreme duress, such as when revealing your religion could result in your death.

29. Gottschalk and Greenberg, *Islamophobia*, 41–43.

30. Karim H. Karim, "American Media's Coverage of Muslims: The Historical Roots of Contemporary Portrayals," in *Muslims and the News Media*, ed. Elizabeth Poole and John E. Richardson (London: I. B. Tauris, 2006), 117.

31. George W. Bush, "Address to a Joint Session of Congress and the American People," September 20, 2001, http://georgewbush-whitehouse.archives.gov /news/ releases/2001/09/20010920-8.html.

32. Men over age sixteen who were nationals or citizens of Afghanistan, Algeria, Bahrain, Eritrea, Iran, Iraq, Lebanon, Libya, Morocco, North Korea, Oman, Qatar, Somalia, Sudan, Syria, Tunisia, United Arab Emirates, and Yemen were required to register at the Immigration and Naturalization Service in person and to report back annually thereafter. The program was ended in April 2011.

33. Moustafa Bayoumi, *This Muslim American Life: Dispatches from the War on Terror* (New York: New York University Press, 2015), 153.

34. House Committee on Homeland Security, "The American Muslim Response to Hearings on Radicalization within Their Community," June 20, 2012, https:// homeland.house.gov/files/06-20-12-Report.pdf.

35. Bayoumi, *This Muslim American Life*, 6–7.

36. John W. Dower, *War without Mercy: Race and Power in the Pacific War* (New York: Pantheon Books, 1986), 14.

37. Jeffery C. Alexander, "Citizen and Enemy as Symbolic Classification: On the Polarizing Discourse of Civil Society," in *Cultivating Differences: Symbolic Boundaries and the Making of Inequality*, ed. Michele Lamont and Marcel Fournier (Chicago: University of Chicago Press, 1992), 289–92.

38. Said, *Covering Islam*, 6.

39. Alexander, "Citizen and Enemy," 298.

40. Mark Mazzetti, "A Secret on Drones, Sealed in Blood," *New York Times*, April 6, 2013, http://www.nytimes.com/2013/04/07/world/asia/origins-of-cias-not-so-secret-drone-war-in-pakistan.html.

41. Bayoumi, *This Muslim American Life*, 8.

42. White House, "U.S. Policy Standards and Procedures for the Use of Force in Counterterrorism Operations outside the United States and Areas of Active Hostilities,

May 23, 2013, https://www.whitehouse.gov/sites/default/files/uploads/2013.05.23_fact_sheet_on_ppg.pdf.

43. Lori A. Peek, "Reactions and Response: Muslim Students' Experiences on New York City Campuses Post 9/11," *Journal of Muslim Minority Affairs* 23, no. 2 (2003): 275.

44. Katherine Pratt Ewing and Marguerite Hoyler, "Being Muslim and American: South Asian Muslim Youth and the War on Terror," in *Being and Belonging: Muslims in the United States since 9/11*, ed. Katherine Pratt Ewing (New York: Russell Sage Foundation, 2008), 85.

45. Peek, "Reactions and Response," 282.

46. Ibid., 85.

47. Ewing and Hoyler, "Being Muslim and American," 85–86.

48. Sirin and Fine, *Muslim American Youth*, 86.

49. Ibid., 88.

50. Ibid., 184.

51. Nazli Kibria, "Not Asian, Black, or White? Reflections on South Asian American Racial Identity," *Amerasia Journal* 22, no. 2 (1996): 77–87.

52. Sunita Patel, "Performative Aspects of Race: 'Arab, Muslim, and South Asian' Racial Formation after September 11," *UCLA Asian Pacific American Law Journal* 10, no. 61 (2005): 63.

53. For a detailed discussion of the role of clothing in identifying Muslims, see Nilüfer Göle, "The Voluntary Adoption of Islamic Stigma Symbols," *Social Research* 70, no. 3 (2003): 809–28.

54. Nasar Meer, "The Politics of Voluntary and Involuntary Identities: Are Muslims in Britain an Ethnic, Racial or Religious Minority?" *Patterns of Prejudice* 42, no. 1 (2008): 72.

55. David Folkenflik, "NPR Ends Williams' Contract after Muslim Remarks." October 21, 2010, http://www.npr.org/templates/story/story.php? storyId=130712737.

56. Bayoumi, *This Muslim American Life*, 148.

57. Spellberg, *Thomas Jefferson's Qur'an*, 271.

58. Donald J. Trump, "Statement on Preventing Muslim Immigration," December 7, 2015, https://www.donaldjtrump.com/press-releases/donald-j.-trump-statement-on-preventing-muslim-immigration.

59. Bayoumi, *This Muslim American Life*, 13.

60. Ibid., 223.

61. Nico Lang, "'American Sniper's' Muslim Problem: How Clint Eastwood Embraces Chris Kyle's Toxic Ideas," *Salon*, February 5, 2015, http://www.salon.com/

2015/02/05/american_snipers_muslim_problem_how_clint_eastwood_embraces_
chris_kyles_toxic_ideas_partner/.

62. Matt Apuzzo and Adam Goldman, "Documents Show NY Police Watched
Devout Muslims," Associated Press, September 6, 2011, http://www.ap.org/Content/
AP-In-The-News/2011/Documents-show-NY-police-watched-devout-Muslims.

63. Jeremy Diamond, "Ted Cruz: Police Need to 'Patrol and Secure' Muslim
Neighborhoods," CNN.com, March 22, 2016, http://www.cnn.com/2016/03/22/
politics/ted-cruz-muslim-neighborhoods/.

64. Liam Stack, "American Muslims under Attack," New York Times, February 12,
2016, http://www.nytimes.com/interactive/2015/12/22/us/Crimes-Against-Muslim-
Americans.html; Uzma Kolsky, "Eight Attacks, 11 Days," Salon, August 14, 2012, http://
www.salon.com/2012/08/14/eight_attacks_11_days/.

65. Stack, "American Muslims under Attack."

66. Barbara Goldberg, "Muslim Doctor Shot near Houston Mosque on Way to
Prayer," Reuters, July 3, 2013, http://www.reuters.com/article/us-texas-shooting-
mosque-idUSKCN0ZJ0RN.

67. Pew Research Center, "Muslim Americans: No Signs of Growth in Alienation or
Support for Extremism."

68. Sirin and Fine, Muslim American Youth, 2.

CHAPTER 2

1. Hamza Shaban, "Playing War: How the Military Uses Video Games," The Atlantic,
October 10, 2013, http://www.theatlantic.com/technology/archive/2013/10/playing-war-
how-the-military-uses-video-games/280486/.

2. Naomi Wolf, "Katy Perry and the Military-Pop-Cultural Complex," The Guardian,
April 16, 2012, http://www.theguardian.com/commentisfree/cifamerica/2012/apr/16/
katy-perry-military-pop-cultural-complex.

3. Rob Walker, "The Magnet Magnet," New York Times Magazine, November 7, 2004,
http://www.nytimes.com/2004/11/07/magazine/07CONSUMED.html?_r=0.

4. Executive Order 9981, http://www.trumanlibrary.org/9981a.htm.

5. Public Broadcasting Service, "Africans in America: The Revolutionary War,"
http://www.pbs.org/wgbh/aia/part2/2narr4.html.

6. Charles C. Moskos and John Sibley Butler, All That We Can Be: Black Leadership
and Racial Integration the Army Way (New York: Basic Books, 1996), 33–34.

7. Black women were not allowed to serve in military roles until near the end of

the war when eighteen black nurses were permitted to serve in the Army Nurse Corps caring for black soldiers and German prisoners of war. http://www.womensmemorial .org/Education/BBH1998.html#3.

8. Moskos and Butler, *All That We Can Be*, 28.

9. Brenda Moore, *To Serve My Country, To Serve My Race: The Story of the Only African American WACs Stationed Overseas during World War II* (New York: New York University Press, 1996).

10. Moskos and Butler, *All That We Can Be*, 29.

11. Ibid., 27–29.

12. Office of the Deputy Assistant Secretary of Defense, "2012 Demographic Profile of the Military Community," http://www.militaryonesource.mil/12038/MOS/ Reports/2012_Demographics_Report.pdf.

13. James Burk and Evelyn Espinoza, "Race Relations within the US Military," *Annual Review of Sociology* 38 (2012): 401–22.

14. When it comes to marriage, the gap between the marriage rates of whites and blacks found in civilian society disappears in the military, perhaps in part because the structure of the military minimizes racial and economic stratification (Jennifer Hickes Lundquist, "When Race Makes No Difference: Marriage and the Military," *Social Forces* 83, no. 2 [2004]: 731–57). Divorce, which in the civilian world has higher rates among blacks than whites, is also lower for black service members. Again, the proposed explanation for this finding is the reduction in stress associated with positive and less-discriminatory work environments (Jay D. Teachman and Lucky Tedrow, "Divorce, Race, and Military Service: More Than Equal Pay and Equal Opportunity," *Journal of Marriage and Family* 70, no. 4 [2008]: 1030–44). The relatively positive effects of the military structure also affect children. Education for children who attend Department of Defense (DoD) schools is standardized and does not have the same variations in race and economic status we often see in civilian society. White children have similar levels of performance in civilian or DoD schools; however, "black students who are enrolled in Department of Defense schools perform much better than their civilian counterparts" (Moskos and Butler, *All That We Can Be*, 101). The effect of this is that the racial gap in education seen among civilians is "markedly narrower" (ibid.) for children in DoD schools. The access to health care also has positive effects, especially for black children of military families. Doctors James Rawlins and Michael Weir find that rates of infant mortality are lower for black families in the military than civilians, and that even differences in rank (enlisted versus officer), which in the civilian world might correlate with economic stratification, do not affect infant mortality because the access to health care is the same for all military

families (James S. Rawlings and Michael R. Weir, "Race- and Rank-Specific Infant Mortality in a US Military Population," *JAMA* 267, no. 18 [1992], 146).

15. Moskos and Butler, *All That We Can Be*, 5.

16. *Nisei* refers to second-generation Japanese Americans. These are individuals who were born in the United States to parents who emigrated from Japan.

17. Brenda L. Moore, *Serving Our Country: Japanese American Women in the Military During World War II* (New Brunswick, NJ: Rutgers University Press, 2003), 8.

18. Tamotsu Shibutani, *The Derelicts of Company K: A Sociological Study of Demoralization* (Berkeley: University of California Press, 1978), 45.

19. Moore, *Serving Our Country*, 76.

20. Shibutani, *Derelicts of Company K*, 35.

21. Moore, *Serving Our Country*, 5; and Shibutani, *Derelicts of Company K*, 49.

22. There were two all-Nisei units: the 100th Infantry Battalion and the 442nd Regimental Combat Team. The 100th was based on an existing Hawaiian National Guard unit, and its exemplary performance during training led to the formation of the 442nd. Eventually the 100th was absorbed by the 442nd. The 442nd served in the European theater.

23. Shibutani, *Derelicts of Company K*, 39.

24. Masaoka with Hosokawa, *They Call Me Moses Masaoka*, 164–65.

25. Nisei women from Hawaii were not recruited until October 1944. Nisei women were never permitted to serve in the Navy or Air Force Women's services (Moore, *Serving Our Country*), 88–105.

26. Moore, *Serving Our Country*, 27.

27. Ibid., 97.

28. Masaoka, *They Call Me Moses Masaoka*, 120–21.

29. By the time the draft was reinstated for Nisei men, many felt that the claim for Nisei rights had already been successfully made, and they often lacked the zeal of the earlier volunteers. Shibutani, for example, provides an in-depth consideration of the breakdown of Company K, an all-Nisei unit formed near the end of the war that was most notable for widespread absenteeism, insubordination, and violence. While strong primary groups among Nisei units earlier in the war emphasized proving the loyalty and competence of the Nisei, strong primary group ties became the cause for inefficiency in Company K, where informal group norms emphasizing protest overruled formal norms of military discipline.

30. Masaoka, *They Call Me Moses Masaoka*, 177.

31. Shibutani, *Derelicts of Company K.*, 98.

32. Michelle Sandhoff and Mady Wechsler Segal, "Women in the American Military," in *The Modern American Military*, ed. David M. Kennedy (Oxford: Oxford University Press, 2013), 274–76.

33. Ibid.

34. Mady W. Segal, "Women's Military Roles Cross-Nationally: Past, Present, and Future," *Gender & Society* 9, no. 6 (1995): 757–75.

35. Lory Manning and Jennifer E. Griffith, *Women in the Military: Where They Stand*, 2nd edition (Washington, DC: Women's Research and Education Institute, 1998), 3.

36. Mady W. Segal, "Women in the Military: Research and Policy Issues," *Youth and Society* 10, no. 2 (1978): 101–26.

37. Michelle Sandhoff, Mady Wechsler Segal, and David R. Segal, "Gender Issues in the Transformation of an All-Volunteer Force: A Transnational Perspective," in *The New Citizen Armies: Israel's Armed Forces in Comparative Perspective*, ed. Stuart Cohen (New York: Routledge, 2010), 119–24.

38. Manning and Griffith, *Women in the Military*, 4.

39. Karen Parrish, "DOD Opens More Jobs, Assignments to Military Women," American Forces Press Service, February 9, 2012, http://www.defense.gov/news/newsarticle.aspx?id=67130.

40. Randy Shilts, *Conduct Unbecoming: Lesbians and Gays in the U.S. Military* (New York: St. Martin's, 1993), 7–10.

41. General Accounting Office, "Homosexuals in the Armed Forces: United States GAO Report," 1992, http://www.fordham.edu/halsall/pwh/gao_report.asp.

42. Bonnie Moradi and Laura Miller, "Attitudes of Iraq and Afghanistan War Veterans Toward Gay and Lesbian Service Members," *Armed Forces & Society* 36, no. 3 (2010): 3.

43. Nathaniel Frank, "The President's Pleasant Surprise: How LGBT Advocates Ended Don't Ask, Don't Tell," *Journal of Homosexuality* 60, no. 1 (2013): 159–213.

44. Brenda L. Moore, "Race in the United States Military," in *Armed Forces and International Security*, ed. Jean Callaghan and Franz Kernic (New Brunswick, NJ: Transaction, 2003), 244.

45. Leo Bogart, *Social Research and the Desegregation of the U.S. Army* (Chicago: Markham, 1969).

46. Brigades are composed of 3,000 to 5,000 personnel; companies are smaller, composed of 50 to 200 personnel.

47. U.S. Army, "Commander's Equal Opportunity Handbook," http://www.armyg1.army.mil/eo/docs/tc26-6.pdf.

48. Efrat Elron, Boas Shamir, and Eyal Ben-Ari, "Why Don't They Fight Each Other? Cultural Diversity and Operational Unity in Multinational Forces," *Armed Forces & Society* 26, no. 1 (1999): 73–97.

49. Gordon Allport, *The Nature of Prejudice* (Boston: Beacon, 1954).

50. Ibid., 268.

51. Ibid., 276.

52. Ibid., 281.

53. Bogart, *Social Research and the Desegregation of the U.S. Army*, 183.

54. For example, Sonia Azad, "Serving God and Country," Medill Reports, March 20, 2008, http://news.medill.northwestern.edu/washington/news.aspx?id=84455.

55. Shahed Amanullah, "Crescents among the Crosses at Arlington Cemetery," Altmuslim, 2005, http://www.altMuslim.com/a/a/print/1986/.

56. Andrea Elliott, "Sorting Out Life as Muslims and Marines," *New York Times*, August 7, 2006, http://www.nytimes.com/2006/08/07/nyregion/07marines.html.

57. Kristy N. Kamarck, "Diversity, Inclusion, and Equal Opportunity in the Armed Services: Background Issues for Congress," *Congressional Research Service*, 7-5700, https://www.fas.org/sgp/crs/natsec/R44321.pdf.

58. Laurie Goodstein, "A Nation Challenged: The Clergy; Military Clerics Balance Arms and Allah," *New York Times*, October 7, 2001, http://www.nytimes.com/2001/10/07/us/a-nation-challenged-the-clergy-military-clerics-balance-arms-and-allah.html.

59. Kim Hansen, *Military Chaplains and Religious Diversity* (New York: Palgrave Macmillan, 2012), 39–70.

60. Carlos C. Huerta and Schuyler C. Webb, "Religious Accommodation in the Military," in *Managing Diversity in the Military*, ed. Mickey R. Dansby, James B. Stewart, and Schuyler C. Webb (New Brunswick, NJ: Transaction, 2001), 86.

61. Department of Defense, "Accommodation of Religious Practices within the Military Services" (Number 1300.17), 2014, http://www.dtic.mil/whs/directives/corres/pdf/130017p.pdf.

62. Michelle Sandhoff, "Religious Diversity in the U.S. Armed Forces," in *A Force for Diversity? The Past, Present, and Future of Inclusion in the Armed Services*, ed. David Rohall (Lanham, MD: Lexington Books, forthcoming).

63. Hansen, *Military Chaplains*, 43.

64. James Dao, "Fitting Faith into the Army: Dress Code Is Keeping Sikhs Who Want to Enlist Out of the U.S. Military," *International Herald Tribune*, July 9, 2013.

65. Department of Defense, "Accommodation of Religious Practices."

66. Meredith Somers, "Obama's Pentagon Relaxes Dress Code to Allow Turbans,

Scarves," *Washington Times*, January 23, 2014, http://www.washingtontimes.com/news/2014/jan/23/pentagon-relaxes-dress-code-allow-turbans-scarves.

67. Mark Silinsky, "An Invitation to Denny Howley, Ph.D. from Mark Silinsky," November 18, 2010, Right Truth, http://righttruth.typepad.com/right_truth/2010/11/an-invitation-to-denny-howley-ph-d-from-.html.

68. Mark Silinsky, "Beyond Diversity and Tolerance: Reassessing Islam and Islamism in the United States Military," November 18, 2010, Right Truth, http://righttruth.typepad.com/right_truth/2010/11/beyond-diversity-and-tolerance-reassessing-islam-and-islamism-in-the-united-states-military.html.

69. Pauline Jelinek and Robert Burns, "Military Class Suspended for Its View on Islam," *Army Times*, May 10, 2012, http://www.armytimes.com/article/20120510/NEWS/205100313/Military-class-suspended-for-its-view-on-Islam.

70. Matthew A. Dooley, "So What Can We Do? A Counter-Jihad Op Design Model," presentation at Joint Staff Forces College, Norfolk, VA, July 2011, https://www.wired.com/images_blogs/dangerroom/2012/05/dooley_counter_jihad_op_design_v11.pdf, p. 5. The slides were obtained and published by Noah Shachtman and Spencer Ackerman, "U.S. Military Taught Officers: Use 'Hiroshima' Tactics for 'Total War' on Islam," *Wired*, May 10, 2012, https://www.wired.com/2012/05/total-war-islam.

71. Dooley, "So What Can We Do?" 7.

72. Ibid., 28.

73. Tawfik Hamid, http://www.tawfikhamid.com/#bio.

74. Tawfik Hamid, "A Strategic Plan to Defeat Radical Islam," in *Topical Strategic Multi-Layer Assessment and Air Force Research Laboratory Multi-Disciplinary White Paper in Support of Counter-Terrorism and Counter-WMD*, ed. Laurie Fenstermacher (2015), 72, also at https://info.publicintelligence.net/ARL-CounteringViolentExtremism.pdf.

75. Hamid, "Strategic Plan," 74.

76. Article 15 is a nonjudicial punishment that is dispensed by one's commanding officer for minor disciplinary offenses.

77. James Yee, *For God and Country: Faith and Patriotism Under Fire* (New York: PublicAffairs, 2005).

78. Department of Defense, "Diversity and Inclusion Strategic Plan: 2012–2017," http://diversity.defense.gov/Portals/51/Documents/DoD_Diversity_Strategic_Plan_%20final_as%20of%2019%20Apr%2012[1].pdf.

79. Edward J. Healey Jr., "Cultural Competency Training in the United States Marine Corps: A Prescription for Success in the Long War," (master's thesis, Military Art and Science, U.S. Army Command and General Staff College, 2008), 12.

80. Ian Duncan, "U.S. Military Struggles to Teach Troops to Respect Koran," *Los Angeles Times*, March 8, 2012, http://articles.latimes.com/2012/mar/08/nation/la-na-koran-training-20120308.

81. Nelly Furman, David Goldberg, and Natalia Lusin, "Enrollments in Languages Other Than English in United States Institutions of Higher Education, Fall 2009," Modern Language Association, http://www.mla.org/pdf/2009_enrollment_survey.pdf.

CHAPTER 3

1. After twenty years of service, service members are eligible to retire and collect retirement pay, which consists of a percentage of their base pay as well as benefits such as health insurance.

2. This description is in line with observations that it is common in military basic training for recruits to be identified by unique physical characteristics (for example, see Kelly Field, "'Hooah!' Freshman Orientation, with Blisters," *Chronicle of Higher Education* 53, no. 6 [2006]: 54).

3. There is an Islamic equivalent of the personalized prayer for the needs or wishes of the supplicant; this is called *dua*. *Dua* can be performed at any time and does not require ritualized movement or a particular format. However, when speaking of "prayer" with Muslims, it is usually understood to mean *salah*.

4. Jack G. Shaheen, *Reel Bad Arabs: How Hollywood Vilifies a People* (New York: Olive Branch, 2001), 9.

5. Elizabeth M. Ginexi, Alison E. Miller, and Steve M. Tarver, "A Qualitative Evaluation of Reasons for Enlisting in the Military: Interviews with New Active-Duty Recruits," Defense Manpower Data Center, 1995, http://www.dtic.mil/cgi-bin/GetTRDoc?AD=ADA293470, p. 9.

6. Yvonne Hasbeck Haddad, *Not Quite American? The Shaping of Arab and Muslim Identity in the United States* (Waco, TX: Baylor University Press, 2004), 5.

7. For example, see Walter R. Shumm, "Willingness to Have One's Children Serve in the Military: An Indicator of Acculturation among Arab Immigrants to the United States: A Brief Report," *Journal of Political and Military Sociology* 24, no. 1 (1995): 105–15.

8. Quoted in Sirin and Fine, *Muslim American Youth*, 101.

9. Pew Research Center, "Muslim Americans: No Signs of Growth in Alienation or Support for Extremism."

10. Sheik/Sheikha is an honorific in Arabic. It connotes being a leader and a religious scholar.

11. *Haraam* means not permissible, forbidden, sinful. Within the Islamic worldview, a distinction is drawn between what is permissible (halal) and what is forbidden (*haraam*).

12. In 1998 Osama bin Laden and al-Qaeda issued their famous "fatwa" in which they called for the murder of Americans and their allies: "The ruling to kill the Americans and their allies—civilians and military—is an individual duty for every Muslim who can do it in any country in which it is possible to do it. [. . .] We—with God's help—call on every Muslim who believes in God and wishes to be rewarded to comply with God's order to kill the Americans and plunder their money wherever and whenever they find it. We also call on Muslim *ulema* [scholars], leaders, youths, and soldiers to launch the raid on Satan's US troops and the devil's supporters allying with them, and to displace those who are behind them so that they may learn a lesson" (qtd. in Foreign Broadcast Information Service, "Compilation of Usama Bin Ladin Statements 1994–January 2004," https://www.fas.org/irp/world/para/ubl-fbis.pdf).

CHAPTER 4

1. Mady W. Segal and Chris Bourg, "Professional Leadership and Diversity in the Army," in *The Future of the Army Profession,* ed. Don M. Snider, Gale L. Watkins, and Lloyd J. Matthews (New York: McGraw-Hill, 2002), 713.

2. Military Leadership Diversity Commission, "Effective Diversity Leadership," 2010, http://diversity.defense.gov/Resources/Commission/docs/ Issue%20Papers/ Paper%2029%20-%20Effective%20Diversity%20Leadership.pdf.

3. When referring to meat, "halal" means that the animal was slaughtered in a specific manner according to Islamic custom. Some American Muslims eat only meat slaughtered under strict Islamic guidelines; others view all non-porcine meat as acceptable.

4. The character Dr. Apu Nahasapeemapetilon first appeared on the television show *The Simpsons* in 1990. An Indian immigrant with a Ph.D. in computer science, Apu works at the local convenience store and speaks with a strong accent.

5. On July 7, 2005, four Western-born terrorists carried out suicide attacks on London public transit, killing 52 civilians and injuring 700 others.

6. Adam Gadahn is a California-born convert to Islam who adopted an extreme ideology and is now a propagandist for al-Qaeda. Richard Reid is the "shoe bomber," a Briton who attempted to bomb a flight in December 2001. John Walker Lindh, who is often referred to in the media as "the American Taliban," is an American citizen who

was captured in 2001 in Afghanistan fighting with al-Qaeda.

7. George E. Reed and Craig R. Bullis, "The Impact of Destructive Leadership on Senior Military Officers and Civilian Employees," *Armed Forces & Society* 36, no. 1 (2009): 5–18.

8. Eid al-Fitr, which is the Eid being discussed here, is a celebration marking the end of the month of fasting during Ramadan. Muslims attend special prayers, which are generally followed by feasting. Eid al-Fitr is also a holiday associated with spending time with family. It is somewhat similar to the experience of Christmas for Christian Americans (though what it commemorates is different).

CHAPTER 5

1. A lay leader is a volunteer who works with the chaplain to provide support for a specific religious group. Activities may include conducting religious services; however, lay leaders are not ordained clergy and so their limitations vary by denomination.

2. Military chaplains are encouraged to offer nonsectarian prayers when performing public prayers outside denominational services. However, this is an accurate report of what Daniel told me.

3. As of the writing of this book, the stated mission of the DLI is to "[provide] culturally-based foreign language education, training, evaluation, research, and sustainment for DoD personnel in order to ensure the success of the Defense Language Program and enhance the security of the nation" (http://www.dliflc.edu/mission.html).

4. Allah is the Arabic term for God and is used by Arabic-speakers across religions to refer to the God of Abraham.

5. *Salaam aleikoum* means "peace be upon you" and is used when Muslims greet each other. It is also used commonly by Arabic-speaking non-Muslims. *Marhaba* means "welcome," and it is rarely used by native speakers.

6. Lesser jihad (*al-jihad al-asghar*) refers to a physical, military war; greater jihad (*al-jihad al-akbar*) refers to internal struggle for personal improvement (for example, a Muslim might refer to the "jihad" of waking up for pre-dawn prayer, meaning the struggle of striving to achieve this).

7. Despite his advantages, Pervez encountered situations that he was not prepared for, illustrating that in-group membership will not erase cultural and regional differences. "I was kinda shocked. I'd say certain things to my team leaders about our religion, and the religious practice in Afghanistan can be very different [laughs]. They're like 'They're not really doing what you said,' and I was like 'Yeah dude, I don't know

what's going on' [laughs]. You know 'cause it's, I mean a very uneducated society; some
of the things that they do it's just like a lot of tribal influences on the things that they do.
The blend between culture and religion, just put it on steroids and that's what you get in
Afghanistan [laughs]."

CHAPTER 6

1. John Keegan, *The Face of Battle* (New York: Penguin Books, 1976), 115.

2. Alex Watson, "Self-Deception and Survival: Mental Coping Strategies on the
Western Front, 1914–18," *Journal of Contemporary History* 41, no. 2 (2006): 247–68.

3. Samuel A. Stouffer et al., "Combat Motivations among Ground Troops," in *The
American Soldier: Combat and Its Aftermath* (Princeton, NJ: Princeton University Press,
1949), 173.

4. David A. Bosworth, "'You Have Shed Much Blood, and Waged Great Wars':
Killing, Bloodguilt, and Combat Stress," *Journal of Religion, Disability & Health* 12, no. 3
(2008): 245.

5. Martin L. Cook, "Let Necessity, and Not Your Will, Do the Slaying: How Realistic
Is Augustinian Realism?" Inter-University Seminar on Armed Forces and Society (IUS)
Biennial Conference, Chicago, October 24, 2009, 18.

6. In the Islamic worldview, intention is central; for example, a good deed done
with ill intention is understood to be a bad deed. Sincerity and intention are seen to be
matters of which only God has full knowledge.

7. The terms "brother" and "sister" are commonly used in the American Muslim
community to refer to fellow Muslims.

8. Pew Research Center, "Muslim Americans: No Signs of Growth in Alienation or
Support for Extremism."

9. A *taqiyah* is a cap or hat worn by some Muslim men. In the United States it is
often referred to as a kufi. It may be worn all the time or just during prayer. Those who
wear it generally do so to emulate the prophet Muhammad who, along with his seventh-
century followers, would have covered his head when in public.

10. "They wish you to become disbelievers as they are, so that you should become
like them. Therefore hold them not as friends until they go out of their homes in the
way of God. If they do not, seize them wherever they are and do away with them. Do not
make them your friends or allies, except those who take refuge with a people allied to
you, or those who, weary of fighting you or their people, come over to you. If God had
so willed He would surely have given them power over you, and they would have fought

you. If they keep aloof and do not fight, and offer peace, God has left you no reason to fight them. You will also find persons who, while wishing to live in peace with you as well as with their own people, turn to civil war the moment they are called to it. If they do not keep away from you, nor offer you peace, nor restrain their hands, seize them and kill them wherever they are. We have given you a clear sanction against them" (4:89–91; Ahmed Ali Translation).

CHAPTER 7

1. Adrian G. Carpusor and William E. Loges, "Rental Discrimination and Ethnicity in Name," *Journal of Applied Social Psychology* 36, no. 4 (2006): 934–52.

2. Bernie Hogan and Brent Barry, "Racial and Ethnic Biases in Rental Housing: An Audit Study of Online Apartment Listings," *City & Community* 10, no. 4 (2011): 351–72.

3. Shahram Khosravi, "White Masks/Muslim Names: Immigrants and Name-Changing in Sweden," *Race & Class* 53, no. 3 (2012): 65–80.

INDEX

while deployed, 102; Eid, 81, 84; funeral (*janazah*), 114; hiding prayer, 51–52, 86, 91; leading prayers, 37, 62; media depictions of, 52; in public, 57, 95, 101; Ramadan, 70, 81; respondent experiences, 51, 59, 70, 73, 116; violence because of, 25

Project Clear, 29, 34–36

Qur'an, 46, 54, 97, 118

Ramadan. *See* fasting
rapport, 82, 102, 107, 127–28, 135
religious accommodation: fear about, 18; military policies, 38–40, use by respondents, 52, 63, 80–82, 86, 90–91, 122, 127
relocations, 48, 52, 80
retirement, 48, 84, 94
ROTC, 86, 98–99, 101, 137

Said, Edward, 20
salah. *See* prayer
security clearances, 55–56
sexual harassment, 74–75
Shaheen, Jack, 52
Shibutani, Tamotsu, 32
Sikhs, 23, 49, 60, 105
Silinksy, Mark, 42
Simpsons, The, 70
Sirin, Selcuk, 21, 26, 61
slavery, 14–15
Sodhi, Balbir Singh, 23
South Asians: experiences after 9/11,

21; history in U.S., 15–16; racialization, 22, 137; respondents, 48, 58, 63, 66, 70, 72, 74, 98, 104, 110, 114
Spellberg, Denise, 13–14, 23
Stouffer, Samuel, 116

taqiyah. See *kufi*
taqiyyah (dissimulation), 18
teasing, 50, 112, 115
terrorism, 18, 23, 73; accusations of, 55, 57, 91; counterterrorism work, 62–63, 73, 105–6; discourse distinguishing between Muslims and terrorists, 19, 136; as epithet, 50, 70, 113; stereotypes of Muslims as terrorists, 18, 19–21, 43, 60, 93, 104, 112, 124, 135
thobe, 22
Trump, Donald, 24

Urdu (language), 46, 92, 102, 107, 140

veiling. See *hijab*
Veterans of Foreign Wars (VFW), 123, 137

women, 28, 31, 32–33, 47
World War I, 28, 32, 116
World War II, 19, 29, 30–33, 49, 116, 135–36, 140

Yee, James, 44